M000033992

TOTTERING HALL

TOTTERING-BY-GENTLY™

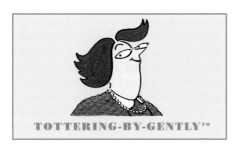

ALSO BY ANNIE TEMPEST

Turbo Charge Your Granny
How Green Are Your Wellies
Hooray Henry
Henry on Hols
Westenders
Tottering-By-Gently Volume I
Tottering-By-Gently Volume II
The Guest From Hell

TOTTERING HALL

Family Life at Tottering-By-Gently

~

Annie Tempest

Published in association with
The O'Shea Gallery

ORION

© Annie Tempest 2001

All rights reserved

The right of Annie Tempest to be identified as the author and illustrator
of this work has been asserted by her in accordance with
the Copyright, Designs and Patents Act 1988.

First published in Great Britain in 2001 by
Orion Media
An imprint of Orion Books Ltd
Orion House, 5 Upper St Martin's Lane,
London WC2H 9EA

A CIP catalogue record for this book
is available from the British Library

ISBN 0 75284 107 6

Printed in Italy by Printer Trento srl

TOTTERING HALL

NORTH PIMMSHIRE

The Seat of Viscount Tottering

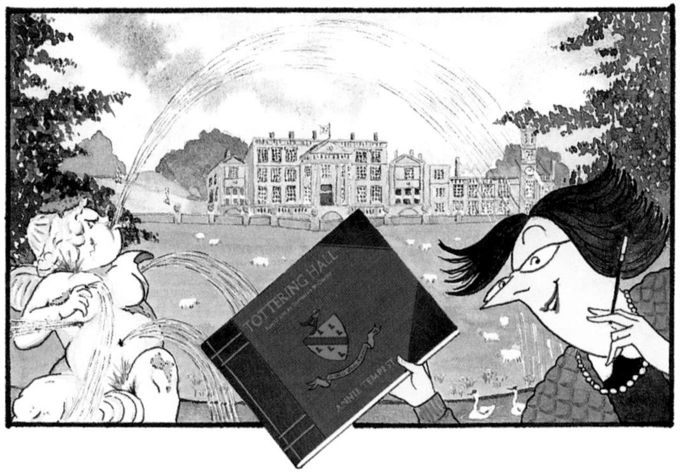
TOTTERING HALL

Tottering Hall is one of the ancient seats of North Pimmshire, and it has long been a name that evokes grandeur and longevity. Many admirers of Jane Austen will have realised that it provided the model for her novel Damenblast Park, in which it was the seat of the illustrious Earl of Invective.

The house was originally adapted from a 12th-century monastery, endowed by Ranulf de Titterung, sword-bearer to the Count Odeur de Brie. During the Reformation, the de Tytterings were granted the house and lands of the Abbey of St Cistern, by a king grateful for their support against the Anabaptists. However, the de Tytterings so delighted in the ancient religious house that they became firm defenders of the old religion, as they remain today.

In 1734 the family seat, little more than the decayed rump of the monastery, was transformed into a palace in the grand Palladian manner by the elegant, if notorious, Henry 'Parsnip' Tottering – later the first Viscount. After returning from the Grand Tour of Italy he determined to build himself a house of the new fashion. There are bills and payments made to a master mason, Courage Mortar. Lord Tottering, however, let it be known that he had been the architect himself, and after 1734, Courage Mortar was employed to survey Lord Tottering's plantations in Barbados and never returned to England.

Many of the fine interiors of the house date from the time of the third Viscount, described by Goethe, while at the spa in Baden-Bagel: 'This tiny man is judged by his fellows a good judge of things: he has the Borghese Potato'. He married the extremely tall Princess Odelwigge. Cardinal Scipio Maserati referred to them in his Roman journals: 'The Principessa

Tottering is like a great cathedral, milordi Tottering like a little priest in her shadow'.

The sixth Viscount 'Spotted Dick' Tottering married Dysunity Blister in 1894, and shortly after became a passionate big game hunter spending much of his time abroad. The Blisters had the monopoly on exporting custard to India and Lady Tottering poured a fortune into the house. Liking, she told her architect, Charles Cott-Blankett, the 'Italianified air of the house', she resolved to rebuild the house with an extraordinary neo-Baroque vivacity, adding two wings with several domes of beaten copper and an elaborate Italianate terraced garden.

By the 1930's the custard bubble had burst and the glory of Tottering had become a huge burden. Jonquil Thimbleton-Finds, adviser to the National Trust, visited the house in 1942 and wrote: 'It was a hideous business: the young Lord Tottering, a friend of my brother Tarquin at Ampleforth, collected me from Rottingbeam station in a car borrowed from his groom; the house is a nightmare of extravagant building of the 1890's, all domed up with nowhere to go but with many good 18th- and early 19th-century interiors and portraits. We ate lunch in a gloomy dining room, used in the afternoons by refugee children for table tennis. The wine was very good'.

The National Trust turned down the house, and Lord Tottering considered selling it to a prep school. However, he took heart when the Ministry of Works removed the domes 'for the safety of the refugee children'. The west wing was pulled down after a fire in 1952 and the house modelled to its present form by Bill Trowser, a pupil of Lutyens. In 1957 Lord Tottering married the Hon Daphne Fitztonic-Gordons, of another of the ancient Pimmshire county families. During the 1960s and 70s the young and energetic Lady Tottering breathed new life into the house: reorganising the furnishings, selling and burning judiciously and removing the garden terraces.

The success of her work is surely to be judged by the remark made by Diana Tailfeather, the interior designer, who wrote in 1980: 'This most delightful of houses taught me a great deal about English country-house taste. Their secret is so obvious and so simple: they do nothing for centuries, but do it very well'.

In this book, *Tottering Hall*, Annie Tempest has collected together some of her own favourite moments in the lives of the 29th generation of Totterings currently very much alive and kicking in her imagination and living at Tottering Hall in the county of North Pimmshire. They are our own dear friends, 'Daffy and Dicky'.

Raymond O'Shea,
Tottering Hall Estate Manager

Researched by Jeremy Musson, Architectural writer, Country Life
Assisted by Lady Crepuscula Harfleight, Librarian, Tottering Hall

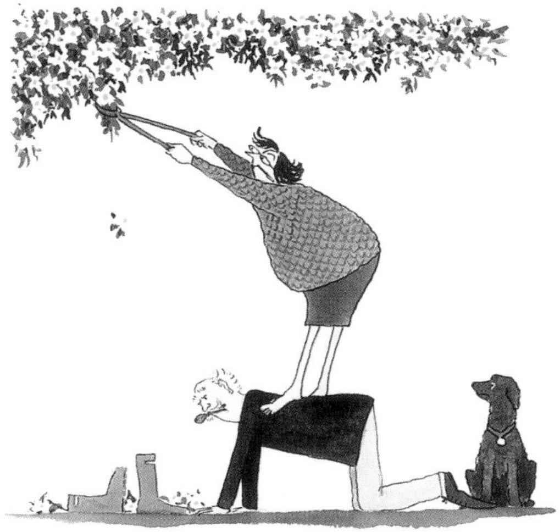

Being supportive...

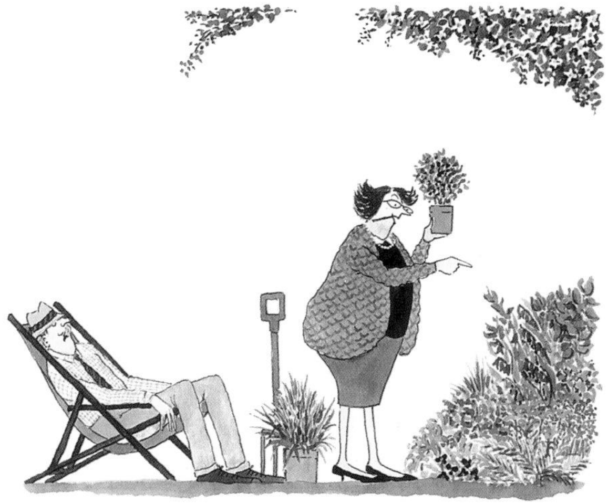

making time to listen to each other...

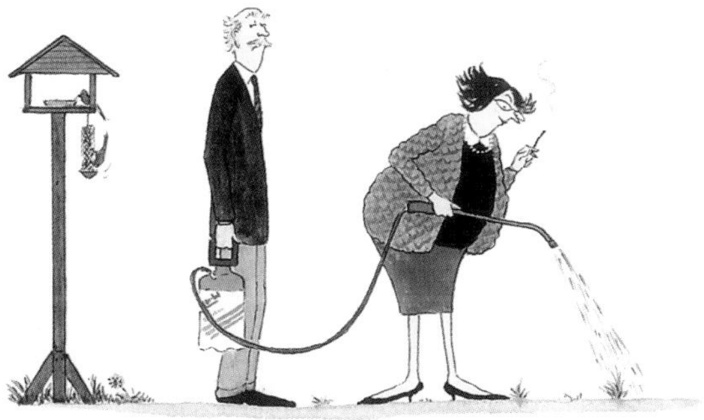

dealing with problems together...

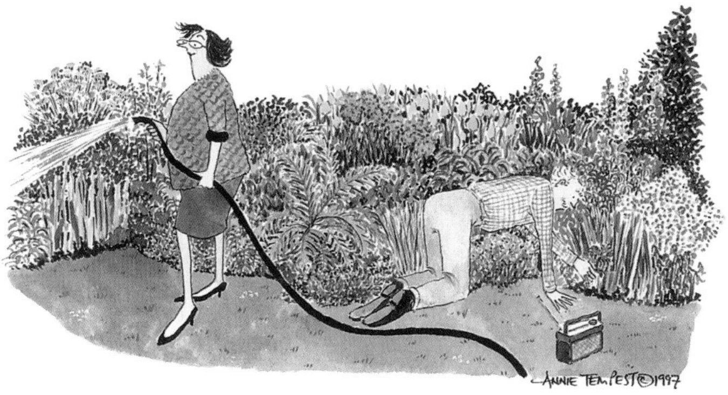
ANNIE TEMPEST©1997

keeping active in the bed department...

THE PERFECT MARRIAGE

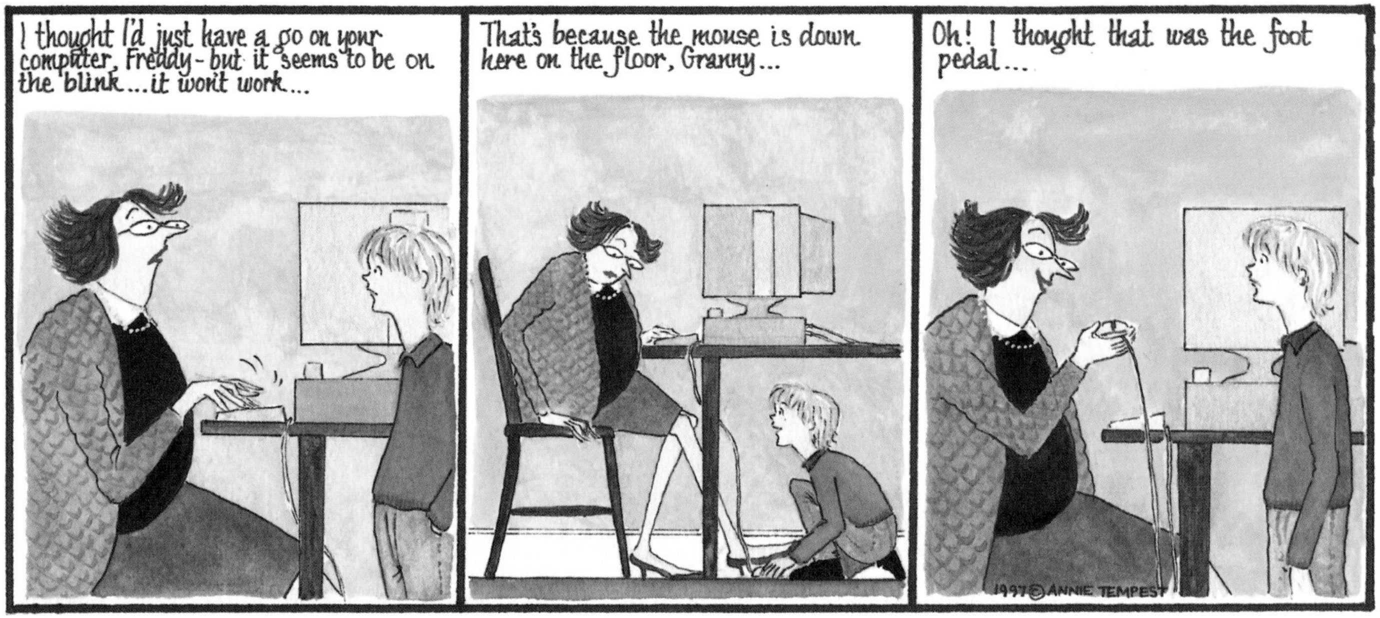
I thought I'd just have a go on your computer, Freddy - but it seems to be on the blink ... it won't work ...
That's because the mouse is down here on the floor, Granny ...
Oh! I thought that was the foot pedal ...
1997 © ANNIE TEMPEST

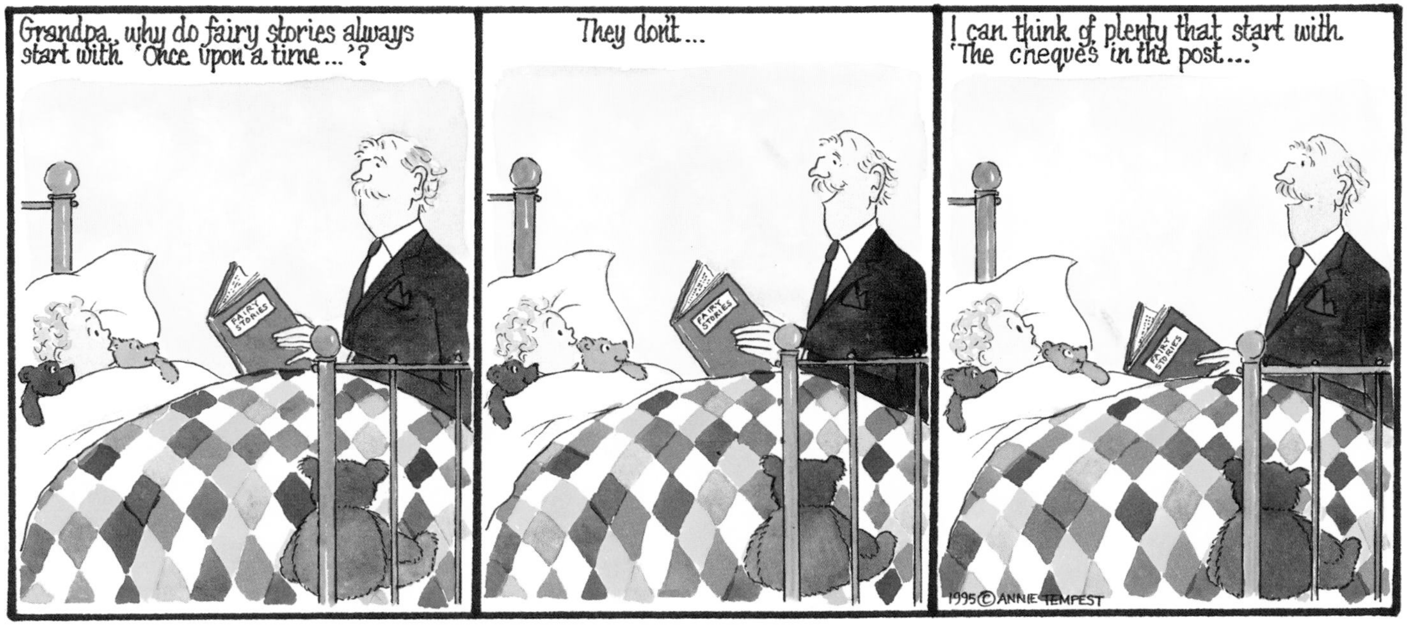
Grandpa, why do fairy stories always start with 'Once upon a time ...'?
FAIRY STORIES
They don't ...
I can think of plenty that start with 'The cheque's in the post...'
1995 © ANNIE TEMPEST

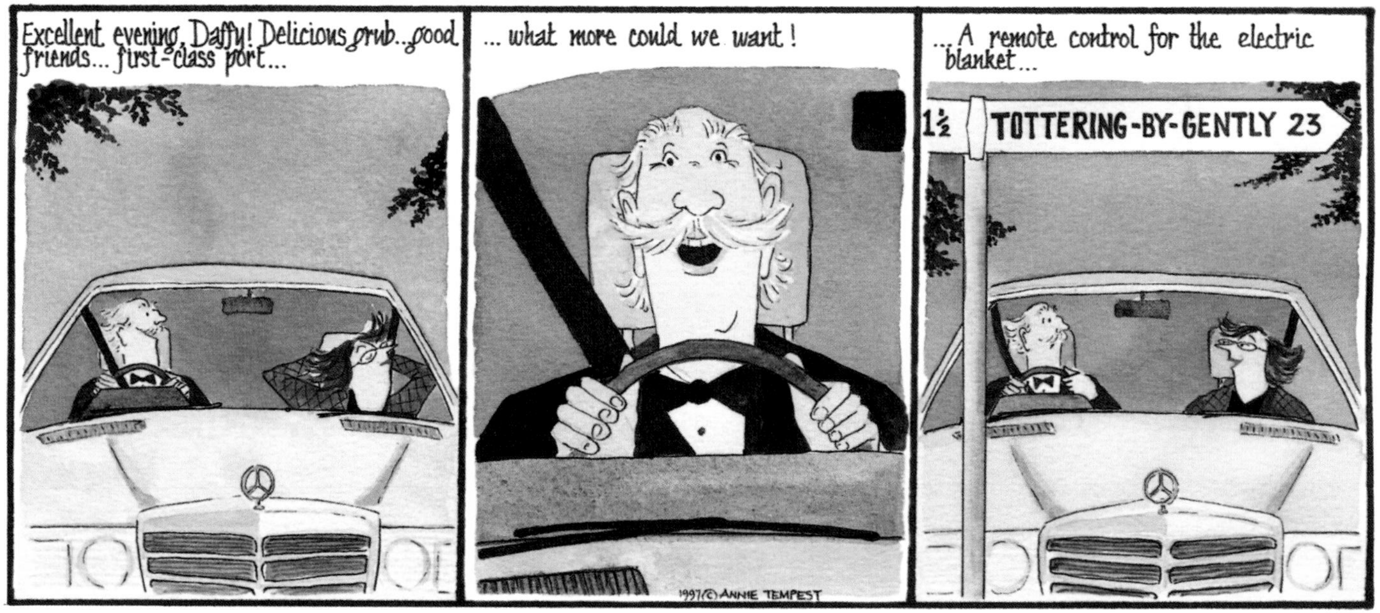
Excellent evening, Daffy! Delicious grub...good friends... first-class port...
... what more could we want!
1997 (C) ANNIE TEMPEST
...A remote control for the electric blanket...
1½
TOTTERING-BY-GENTLY 23

THE WHO'S DRIVING TONIGHT DEBATE

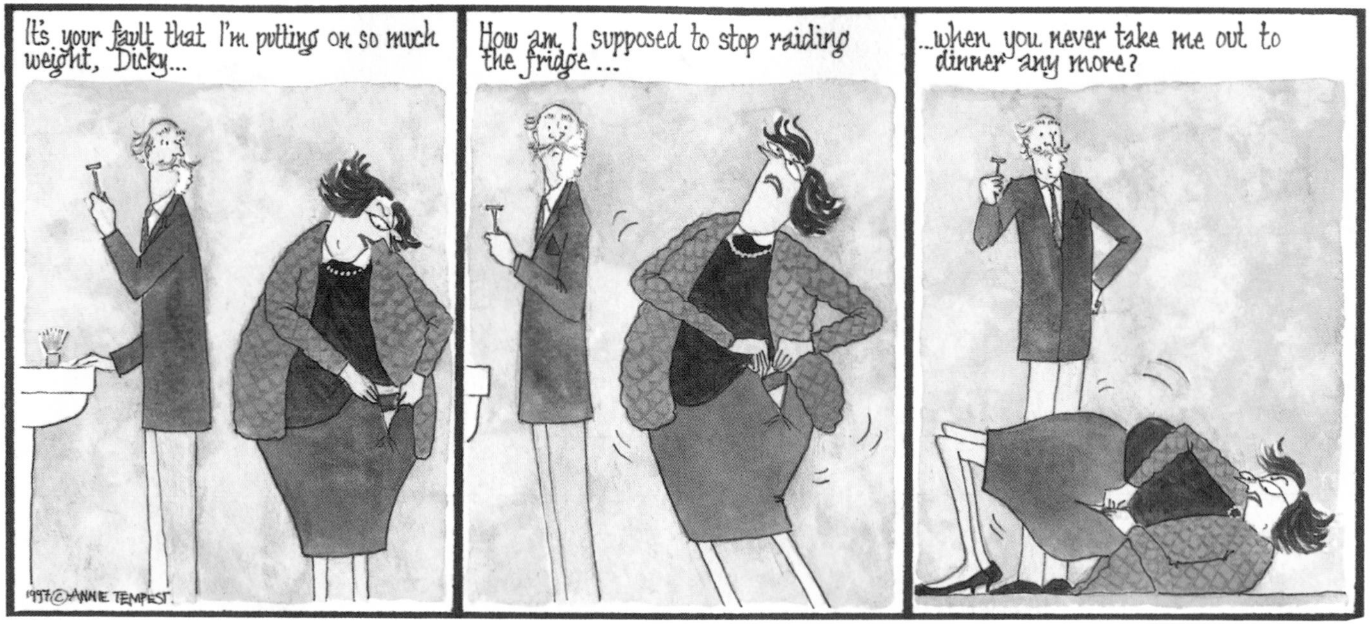
It's your fault that I'm putting on so much weight, Dicky...
1997 © ANNIE TEMPEST.
How am I supposed to stop raiding the fridge...
...when you never take me out to dinner any more?

COMFORT FOOD

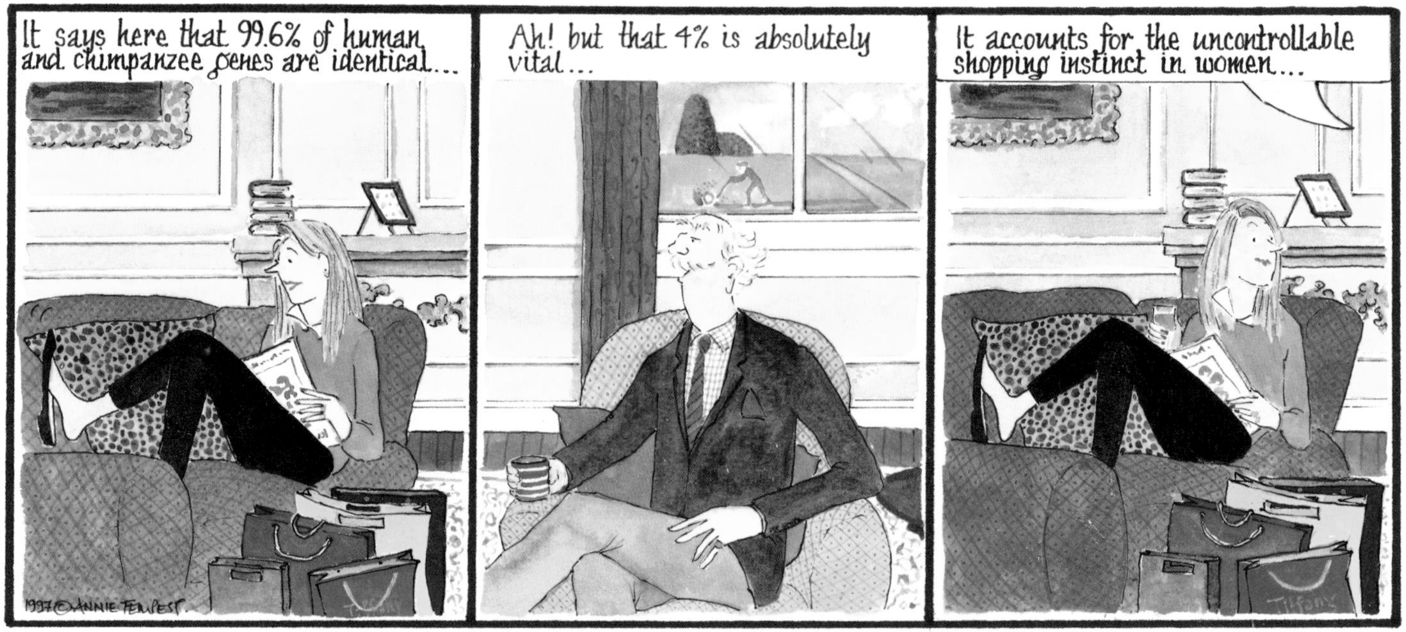
It says here that 99.6% of human and chimpanzee genes are identical...
Ah! but that 4% is absolutely vital...
It accounts for the uncontrollable shopping instinct in women...
1997 © ANNIE TEMPEST

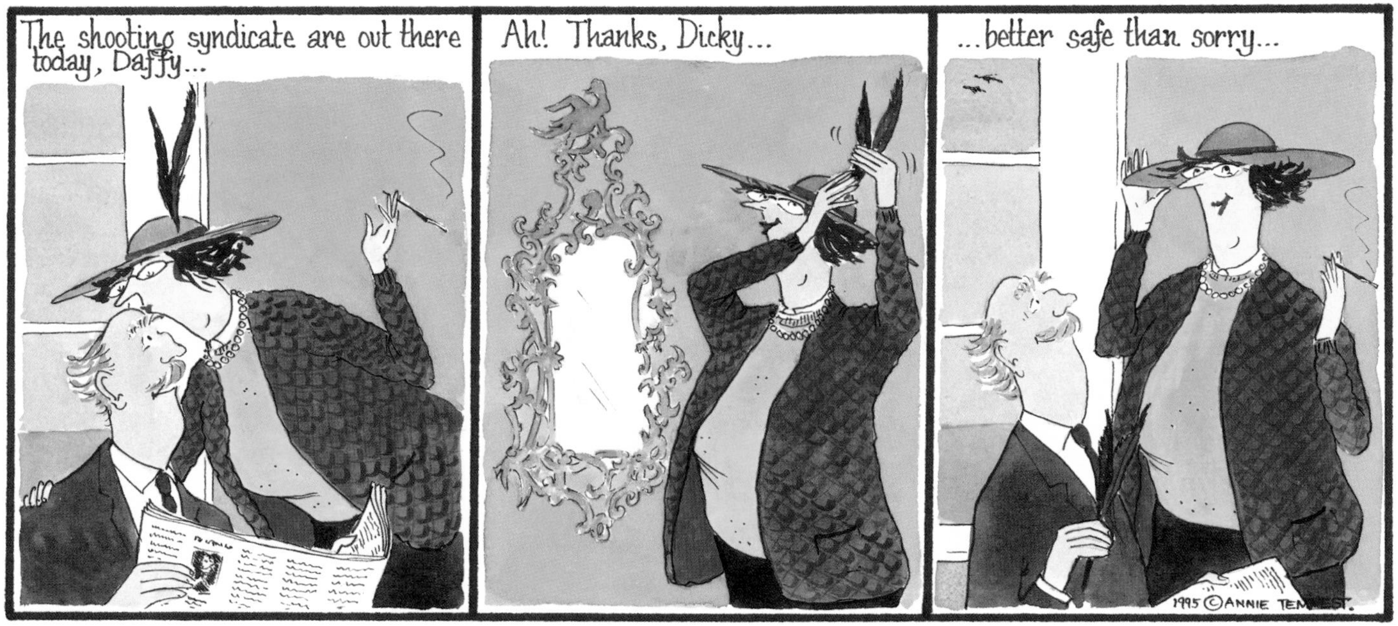
The shooting syndicate are out there today, Daffy...
Ah! Thanks, Dicky...
...better safe than sorry...
1995 © ANNIE TEMPEST.

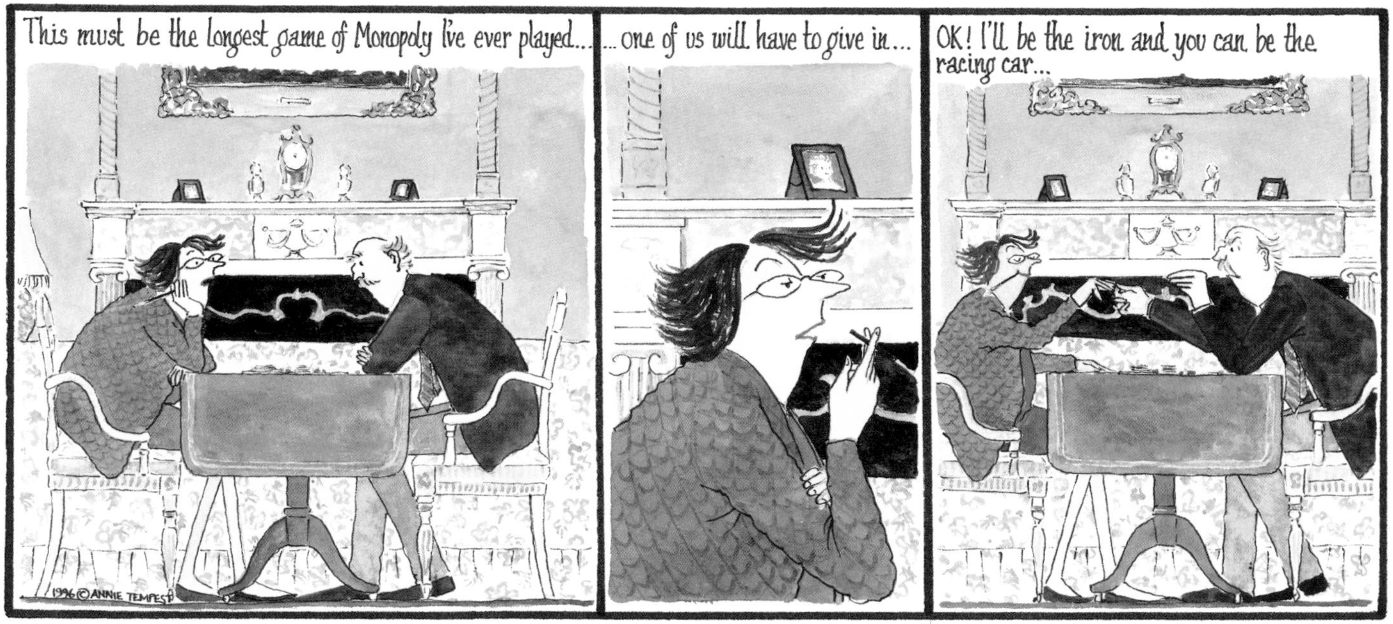
This must be the longest game of Monopoly I've ever played...
...one of us will have to give in...
OK! I'll be the iron and you can be the racing car...
1996 © ANNIE TEMPEST

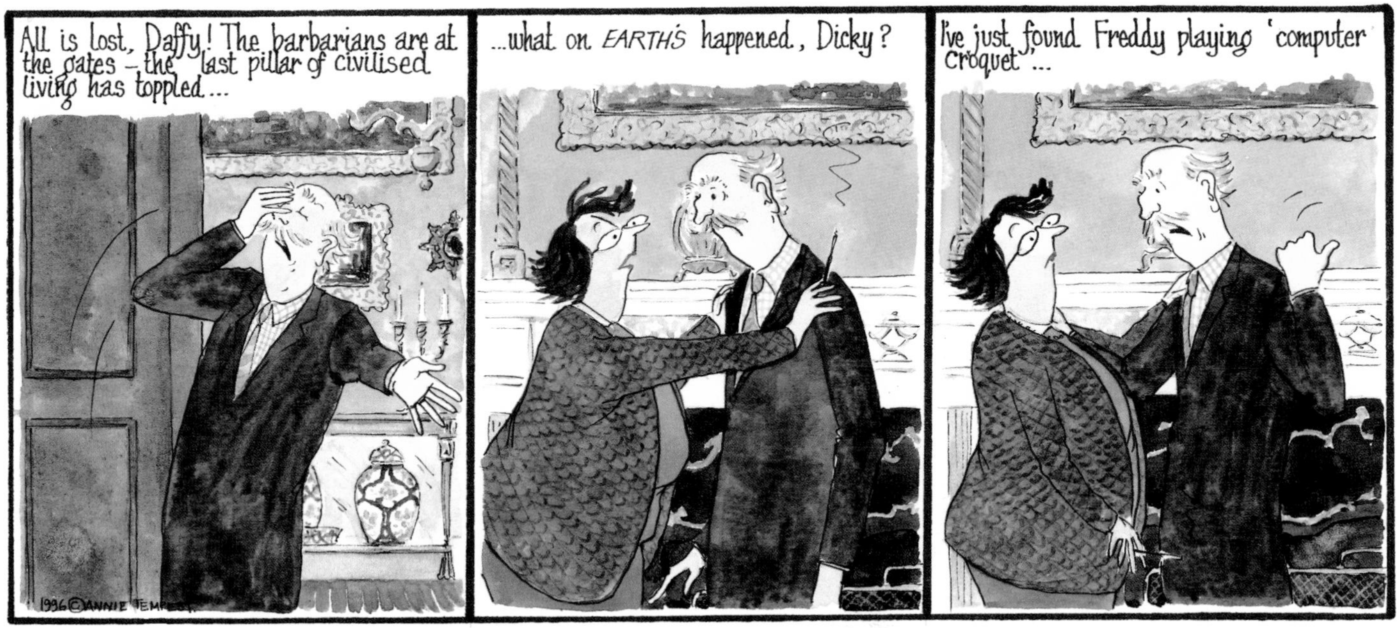
All is lost, Daffy! The barbarians are at the gates – the last pillar of civilised living has toppled ...
1996 © ANNIE TEMPEST
...what on EARTH'S happened, Dicky?
I've just found Freddy playing 'computer croquet' ...

1995© ANNIE TEMPEST.

"You look fine as you are – now come downstairs – it's 8 o'clock. Time to leave…"

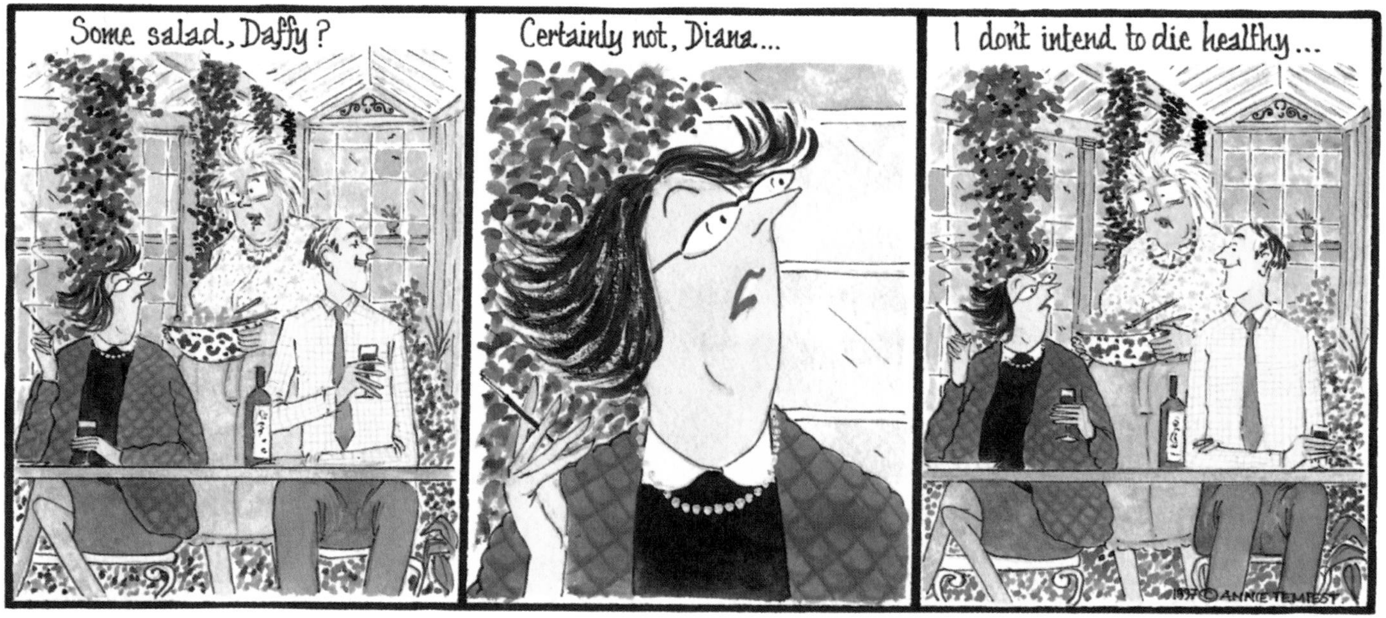
Some salad, Daffy?
Certainly not, Diana....
I don't intend to die healthy...
1997 © ANNIE TEMPEST

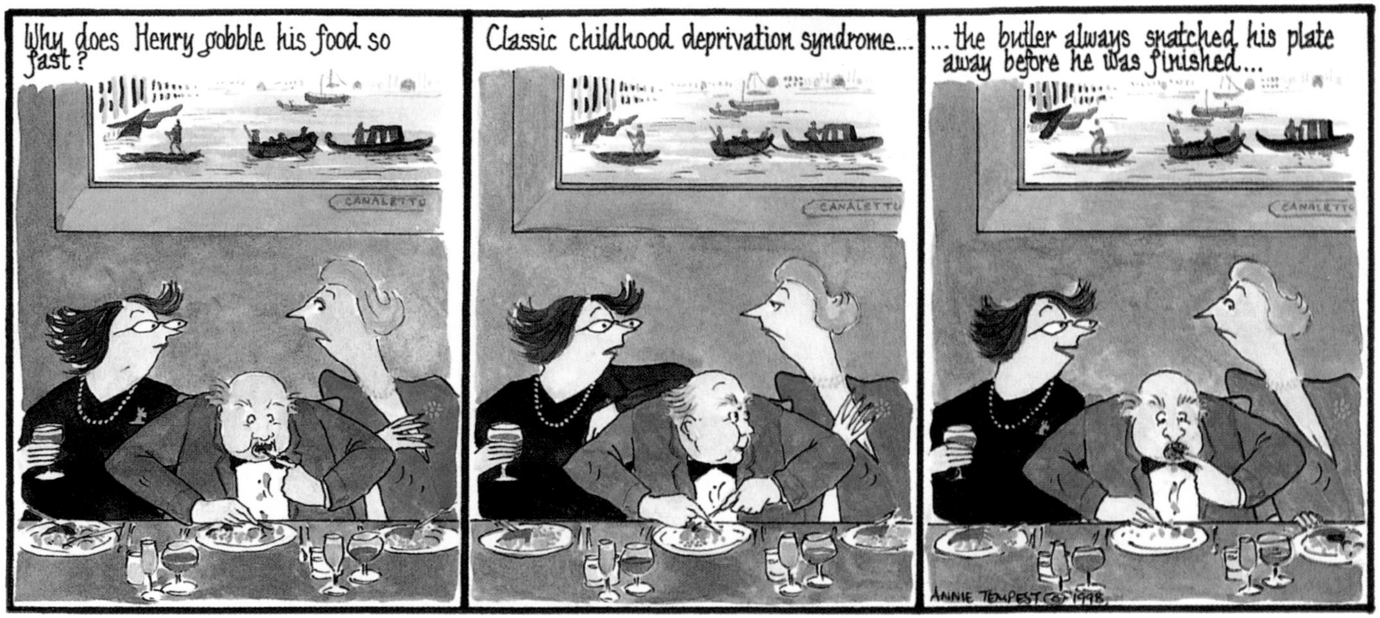
Why does Henry gobble his food so fast?
CANALETTO
Classic childhood deprivation syndrome...
CANALETTO
... the butler always snatched his plate away before he was finished...
CANALETTO
ANNIE TEMPEST © 1998

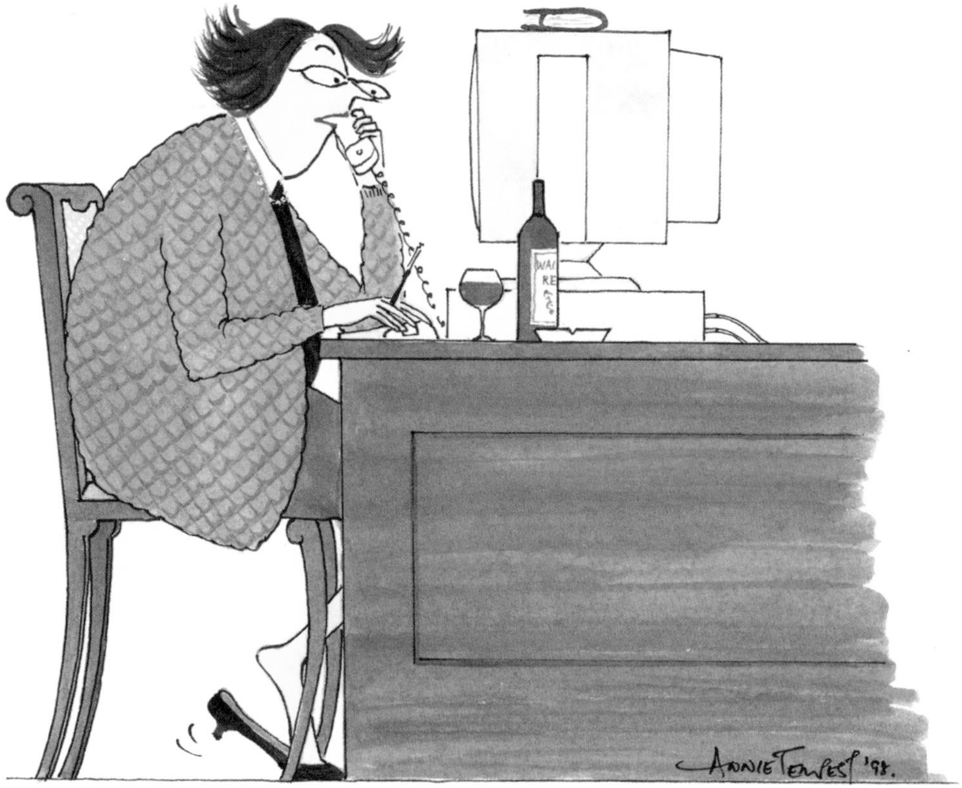
ANNIE TEMPEST '98

"I hope you've got plenty of disc space, darling - I've accidentally faxed you the World Wide Web instead of my chocolate mousse recipe..."

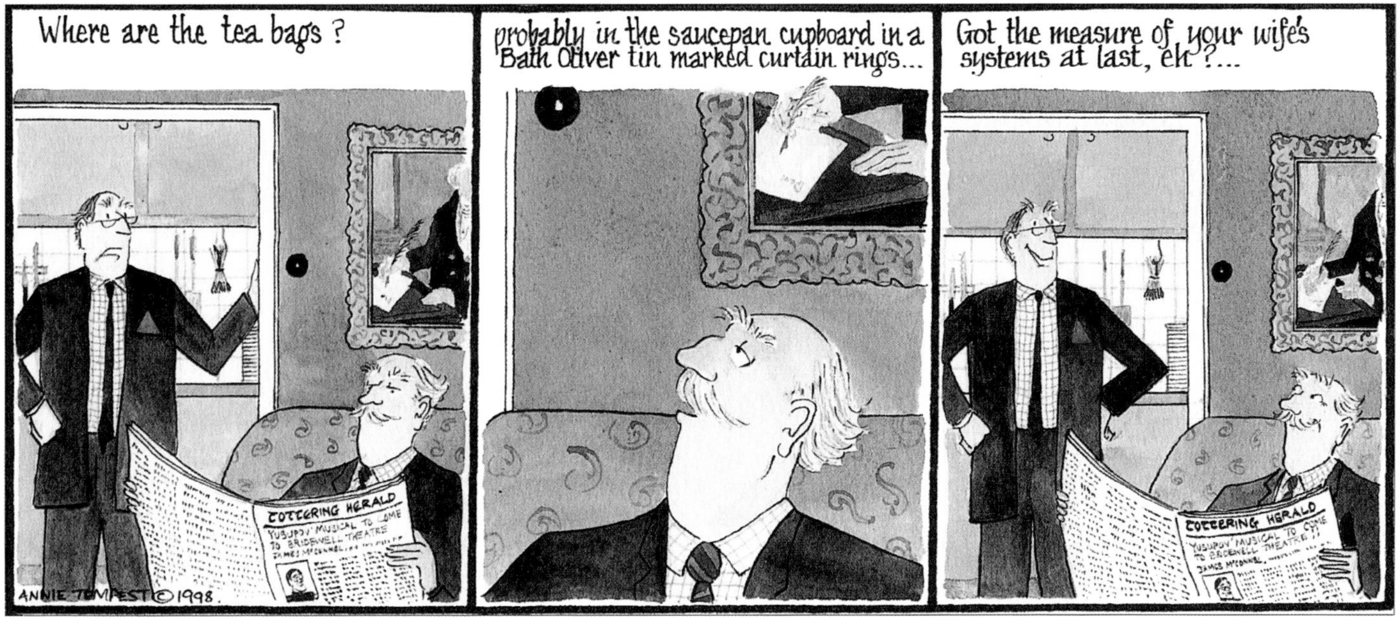
Where are the tea bags ?
COTTERING HERALD
ANNIE TEMPEST © 1998.
probably in the saucepan cupboard in a Bath Oliver tin marked curtain rings...
Got the measure of your wife's systems at last, eh ?...
COTTERING HERALD

"YOU CAN'T EXPECT ME TO BE IN PERFECT SHAPE YET — I'VE JUST HAD A GRANDCHILD..."

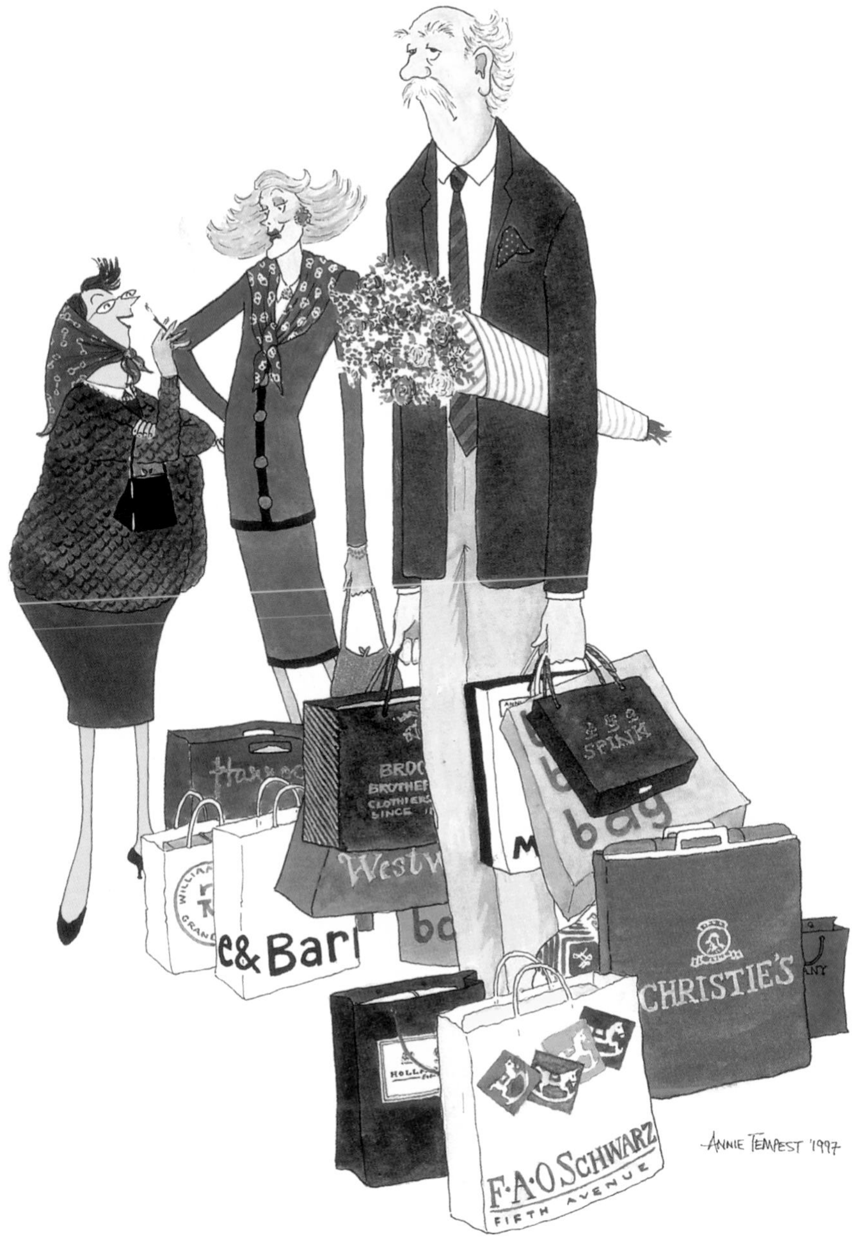
SPINK
bag
CHRISTIE'S
F·A·O SCHWARZ
FIFTH AVENUE
ANNIE TEMPEST 1997

ENJOYING ONES WIFES HOBBIES...

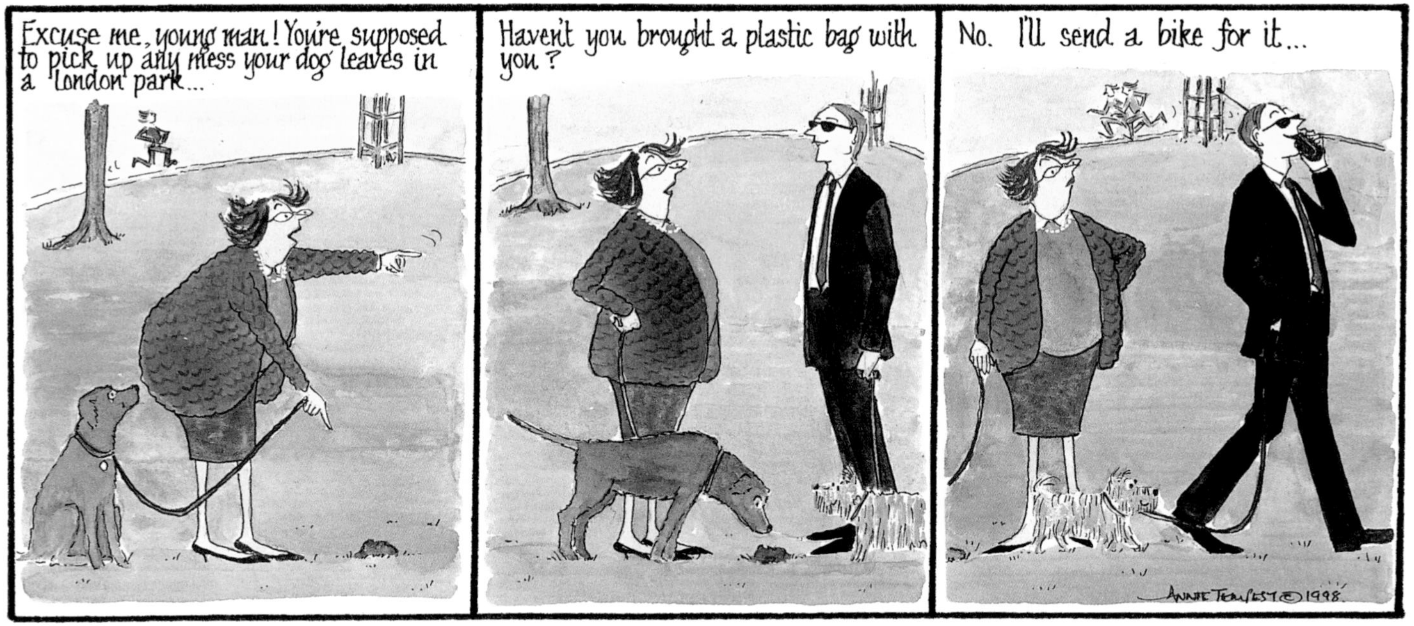
Excuse me, young man! You're supposed to pick up any mess your dog leaves in a London park...
Haven't you brought a plastic bag with you?
No. I'll send a bike for it...
ANNIE TEMPEST © 1998

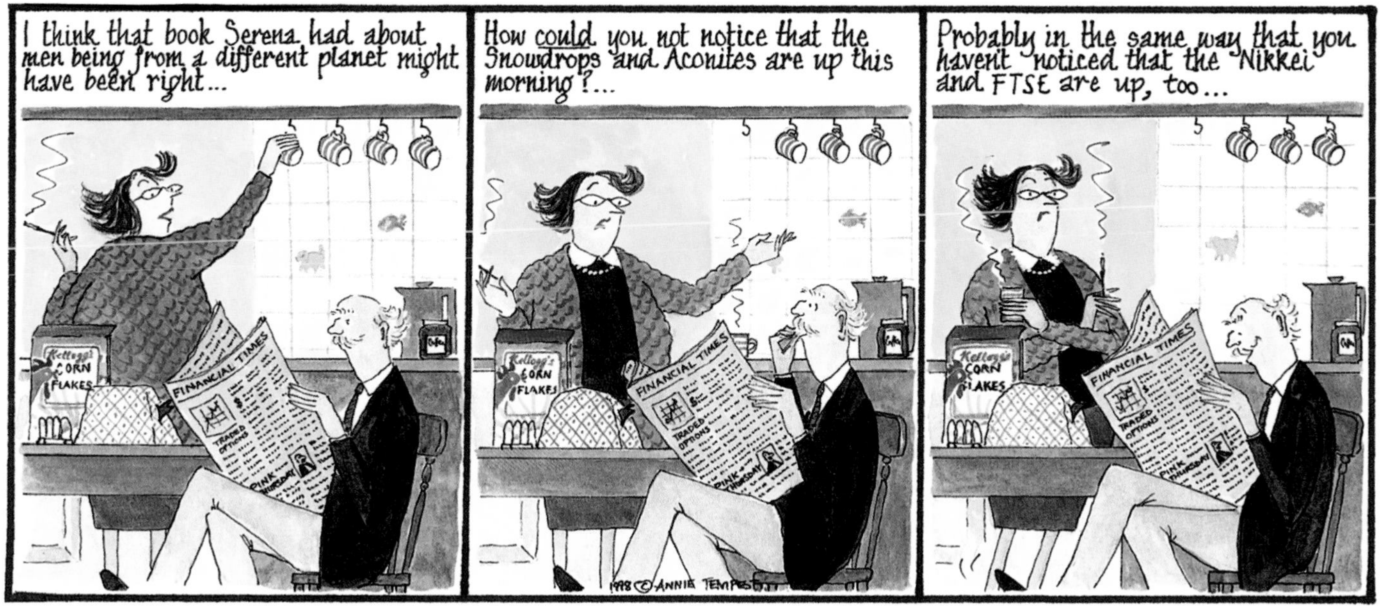
I think that book Serena had about men being from a different planet might have been right...
How could you not notice that the Snowdrops and Aconites are up this morning?...
Probably in the same way that you haven't noticed that the Nikkei and FTSE are up, too...
1998 © ANNIE TEMPEST

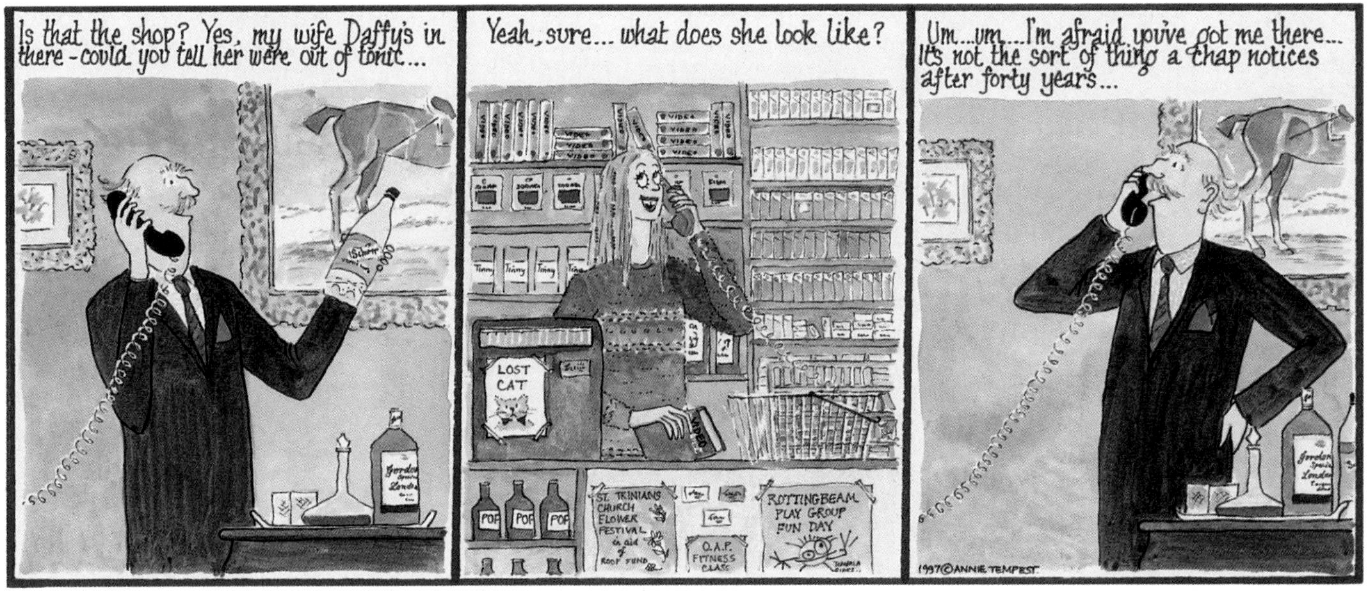
Is that the shop? Yes, my wife Daffy's in there - could you tell her we're out of tonic....
Yeah, sure... what does she look like?
LOST CAT
VIDEO
POP
ST. TRINIANS CHURCH FLOWER FESTIVAL in aid of ROOF FUND
O.A.P. FITNESS CLASS
ROTTINGBEAM PLAY GROUP FUN DAY
Um...um....I'm afraid you've got me there... It's not the sort of thing a chap notices after forty years...
1997© ANNIE TEMPEST

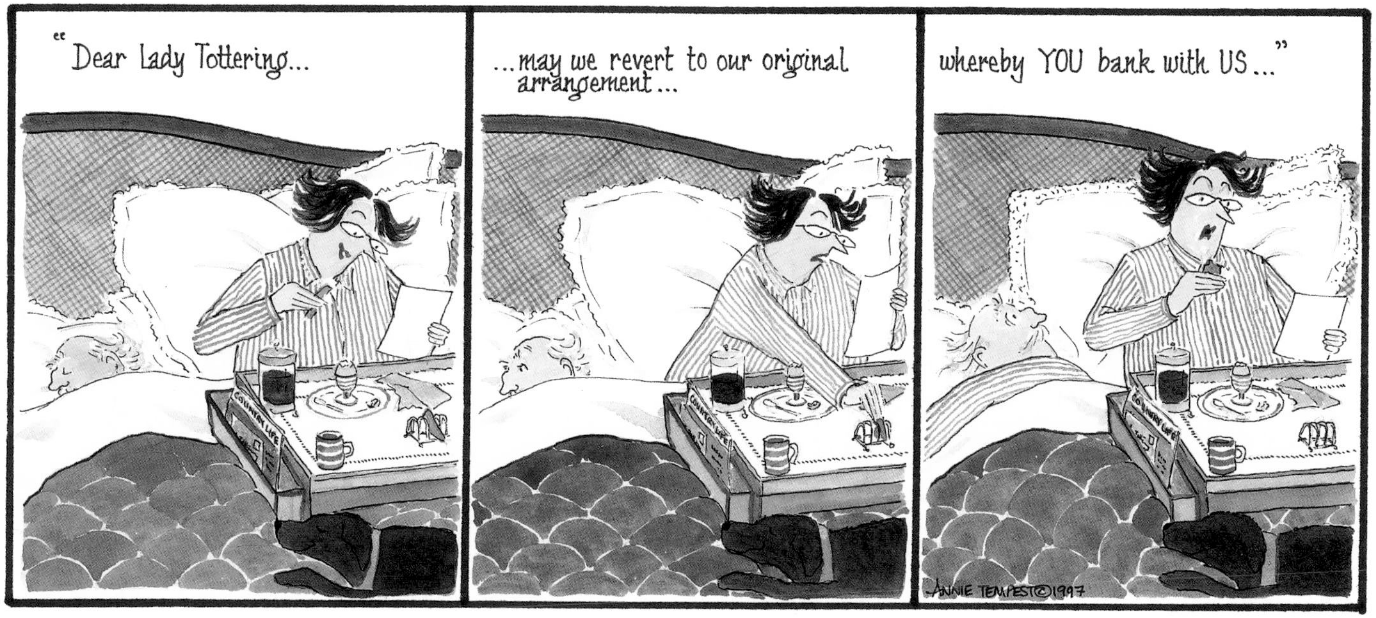
"Dear Lady Tottering...
...may we revert to our original arrangement...
whereby YOU bank with US..."
ANNIE TEMPEST © 1997

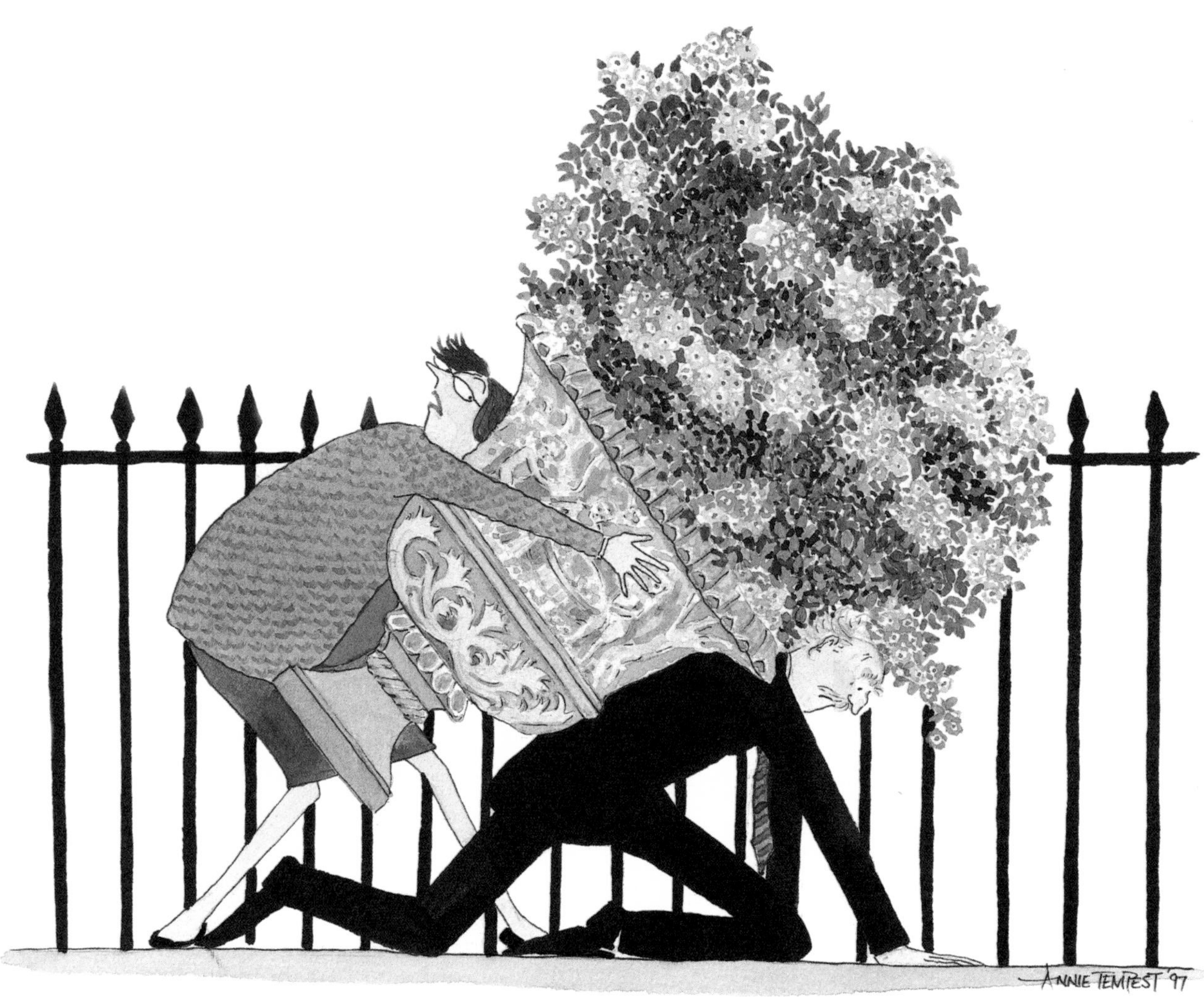
ANNIE TEMPEST '97

"I know I said I was only going to look but it's a woman's prerogative to change her mind, darling..."

GRANDCHILDREN...

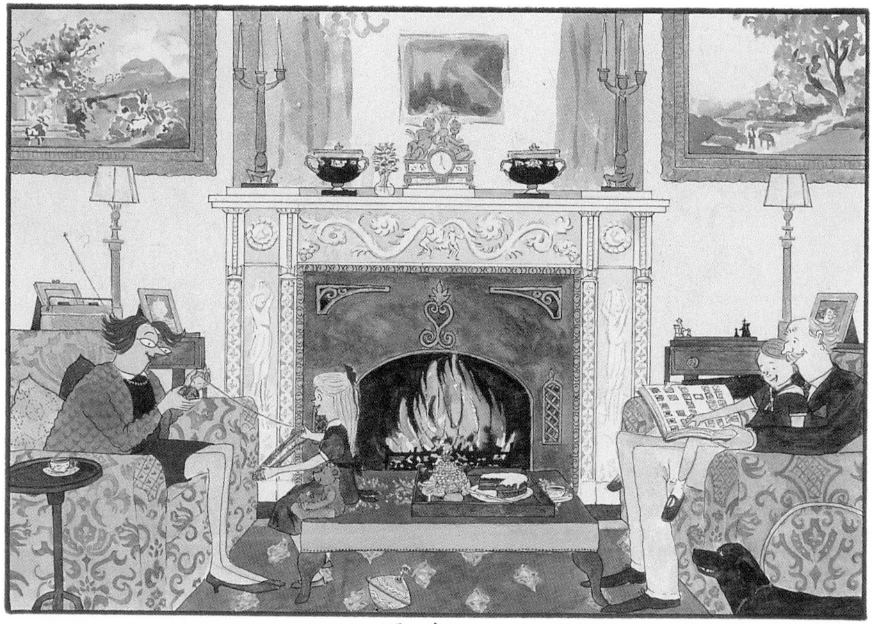

The dream...

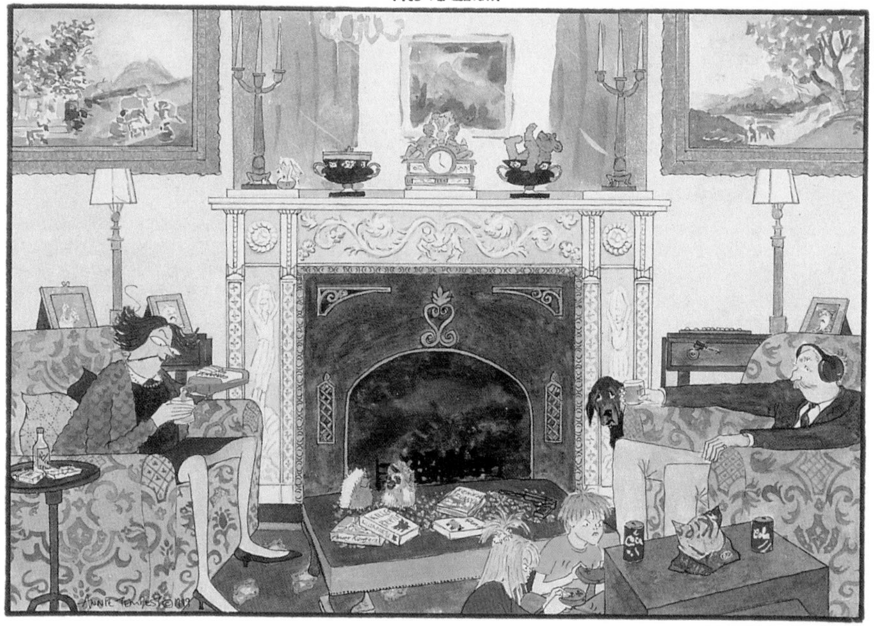

The reality...

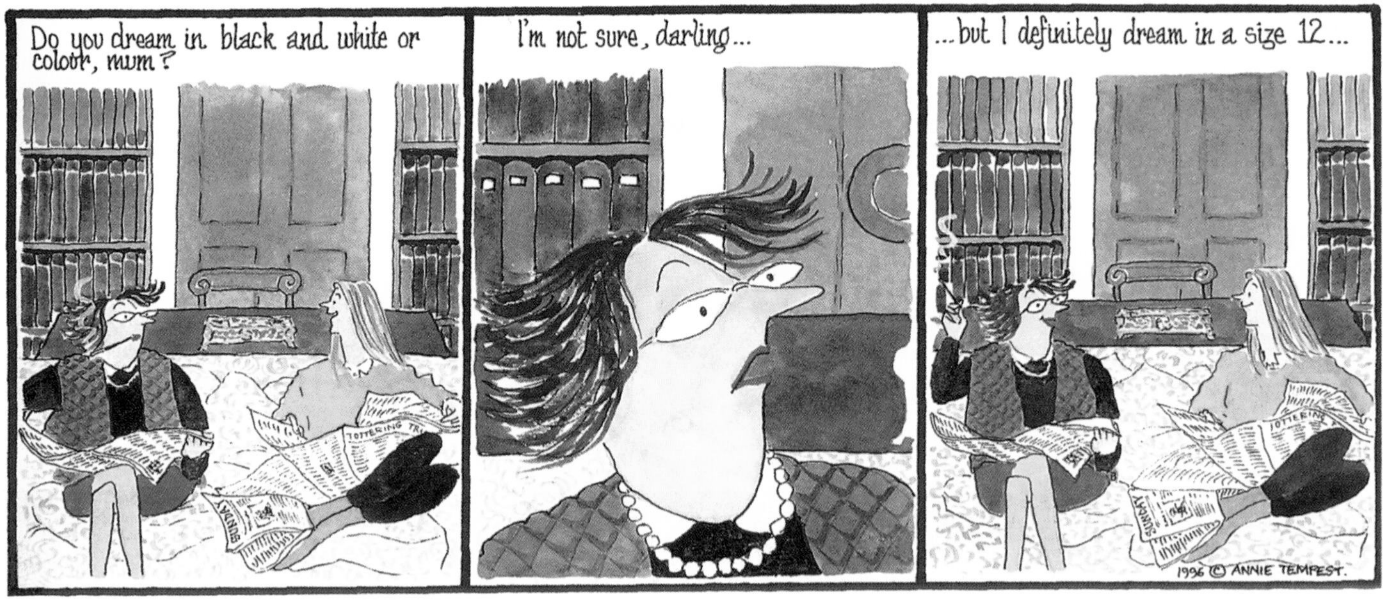
Do you dream in black and white or colour, mum?
I'm not sure, darling...
...but I definitely dream in a size 12...
1996 © ANNIE TEMPEST.

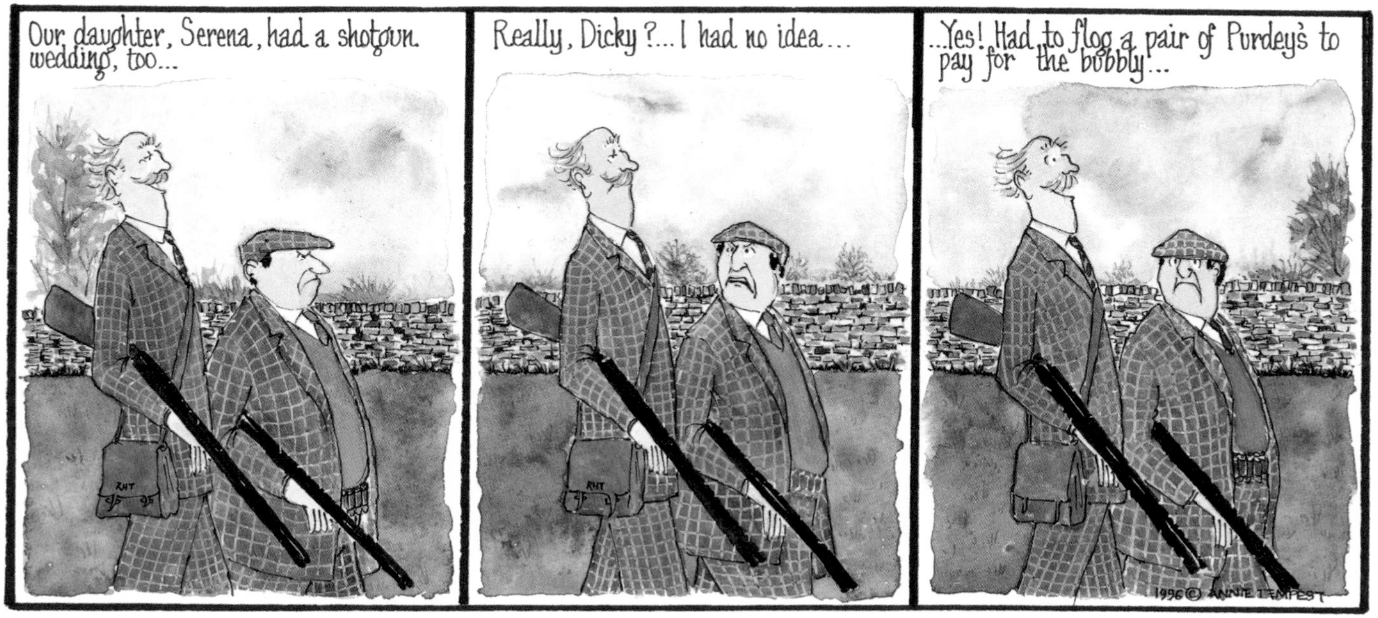
Our daughter, Serena, had a shotgun wedding, too...
Really, Dicky?... I had no idea...
...Yes! Had to flog a pair of Purdey's to pay for the bubbly...
1996 © ANNIE TEMPEST

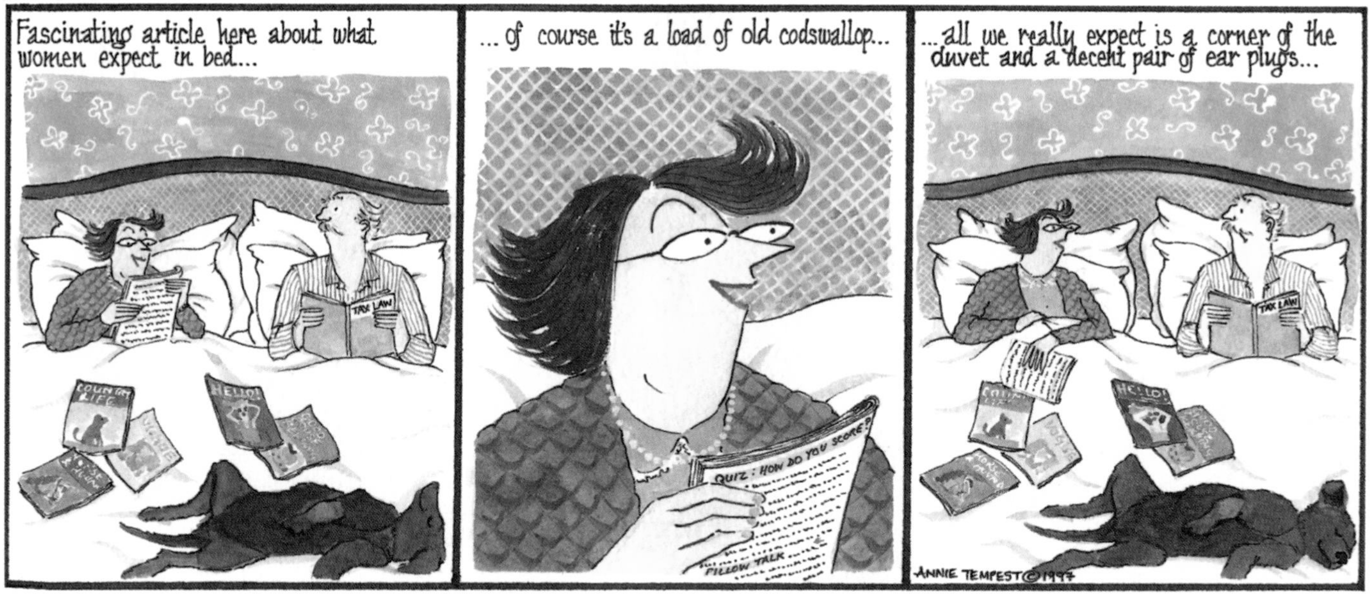
Fascinating article here about what women expect in bed....
TAX LAW
HELLO!
... of course it's a load of old codswallop...
QUIZ: HOW DO YOU SCORE?
PILLOW TALK
...all we really expect is a corner of the duvet and a decent pair of ear plugs...
TAX LAW
HELLO!
ANNIE TEMPEST © 1997

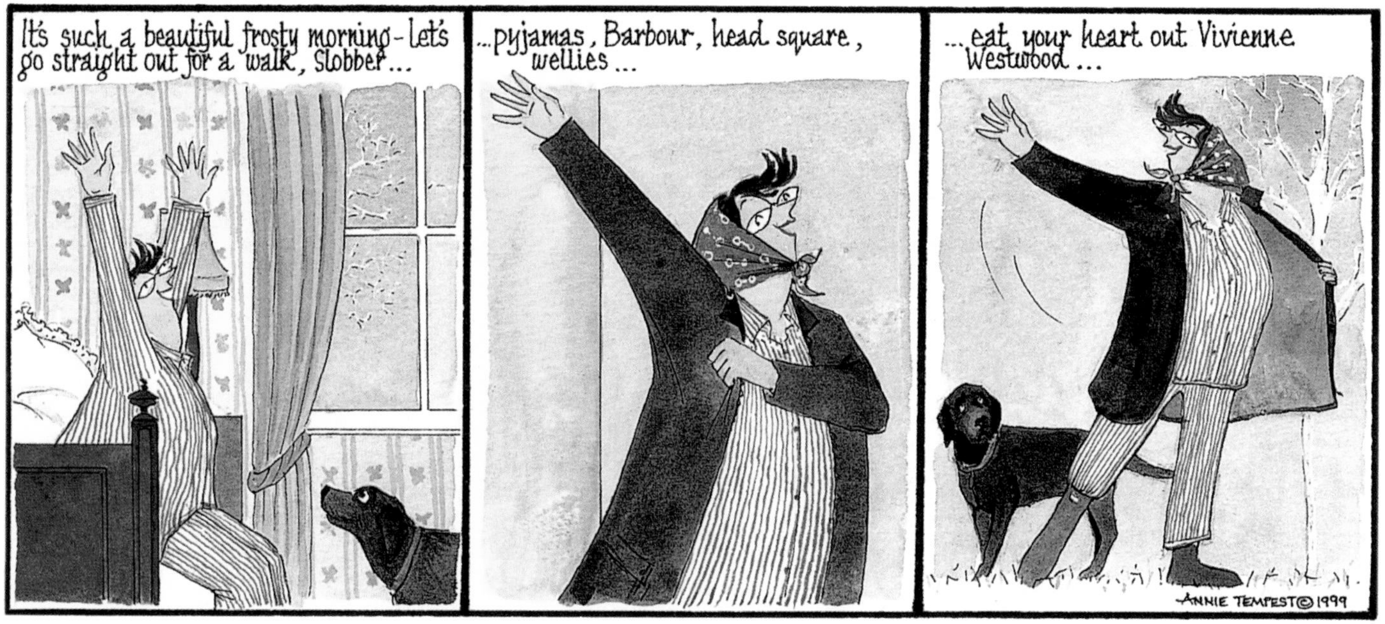
It's such a beautiful frosty morning - let's go straight out for a walk, Slobber...
...pyjamas, Barbour, head square, wellies...
...eat your heart out Vivienne Westwood...
ANNIE TEMPEST © 1999

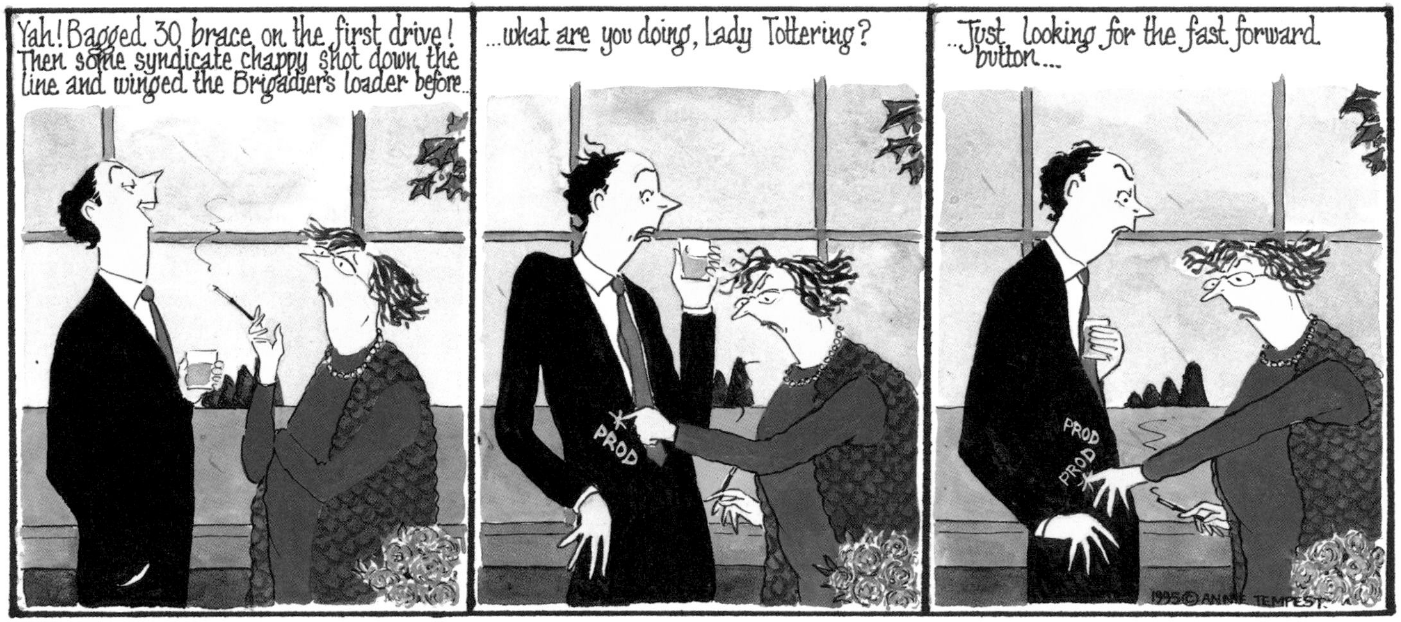
Yah! Bagged 30 brace on the first drive! Then some syndicate chappy shot down the line and winged the Brigadier's loader before...
...what are you doing, Lady Tottering?
PROD
...Just looking for the fast forward button....
PROD
PROD
1995 © ANNIE TEMPEST.

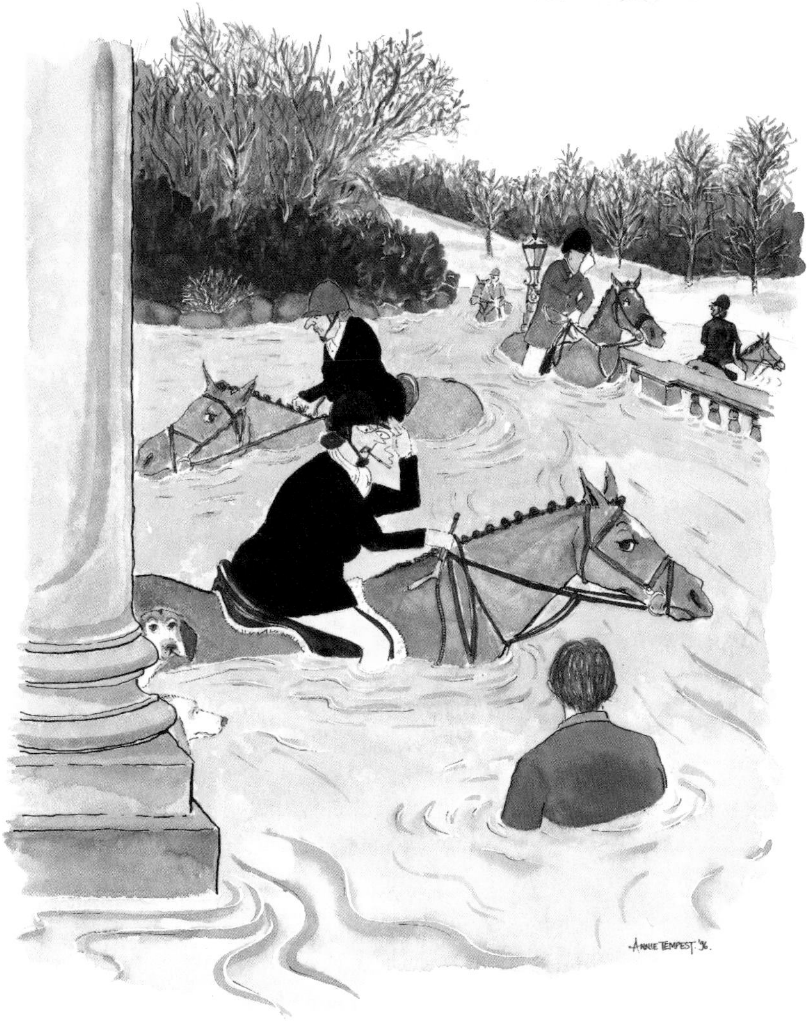
ANNIE TEMPEST '96.

"I can't believe you're cancelling a day's hunting over a few showers..."

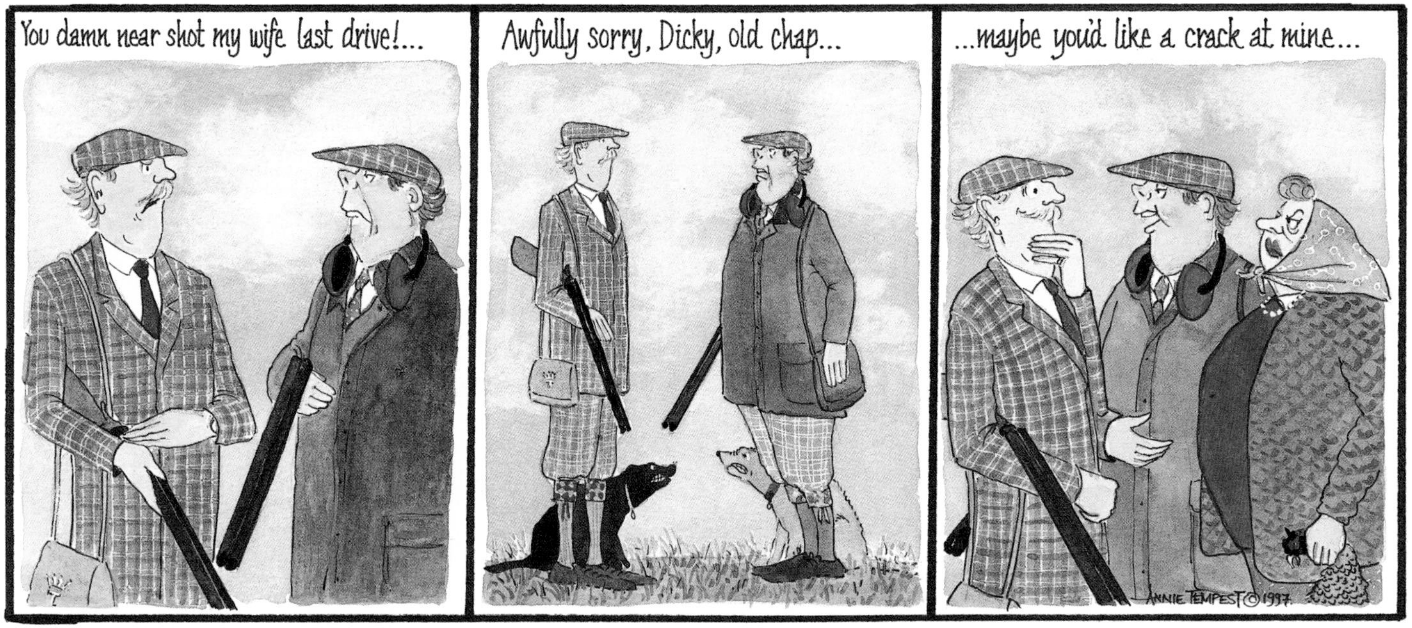
You damn near shot my wife last drive!...
Awfully sorry, Dicky, old chap...
...maybe you'd like a crack at mine...
ANNIE TEMPEST © 1997

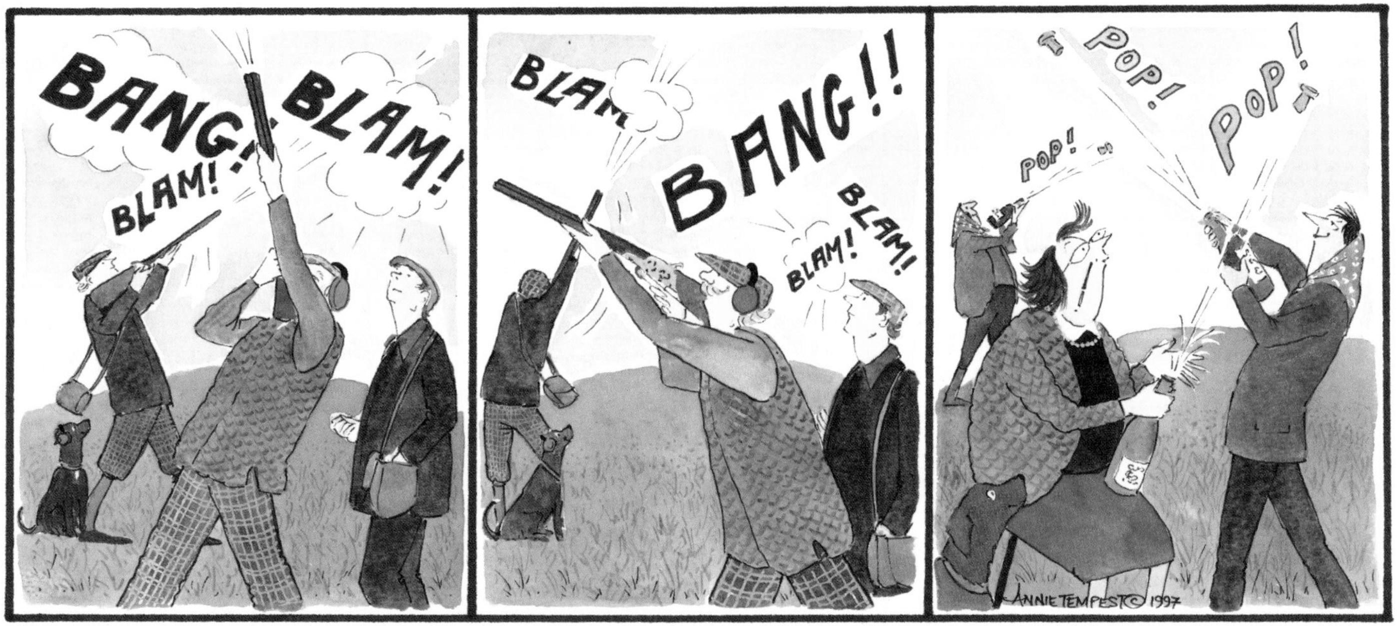
BANG!
BLAM!
BLAM!
BLAM
BANG!!
BLAM!
BLAM!
POP!
POP!
POP!
POP!
ANNIE TEMPEST © 1997

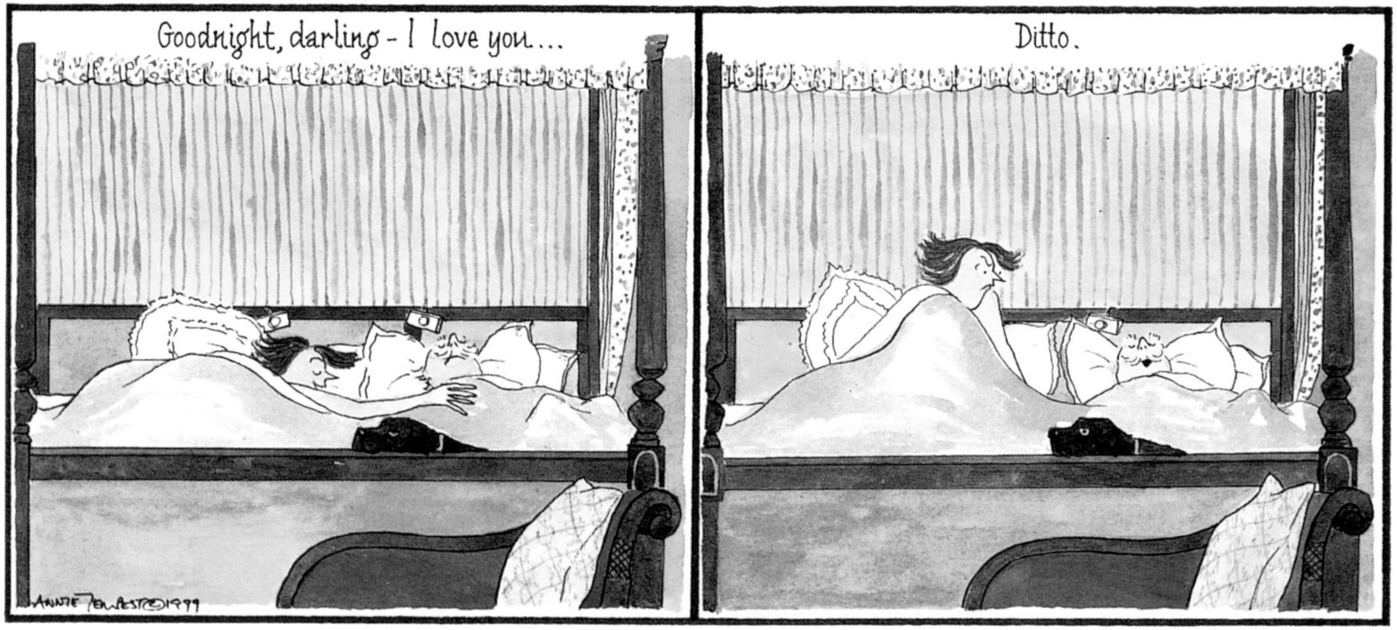
Goodnight, darling - I love you...
Ditto.

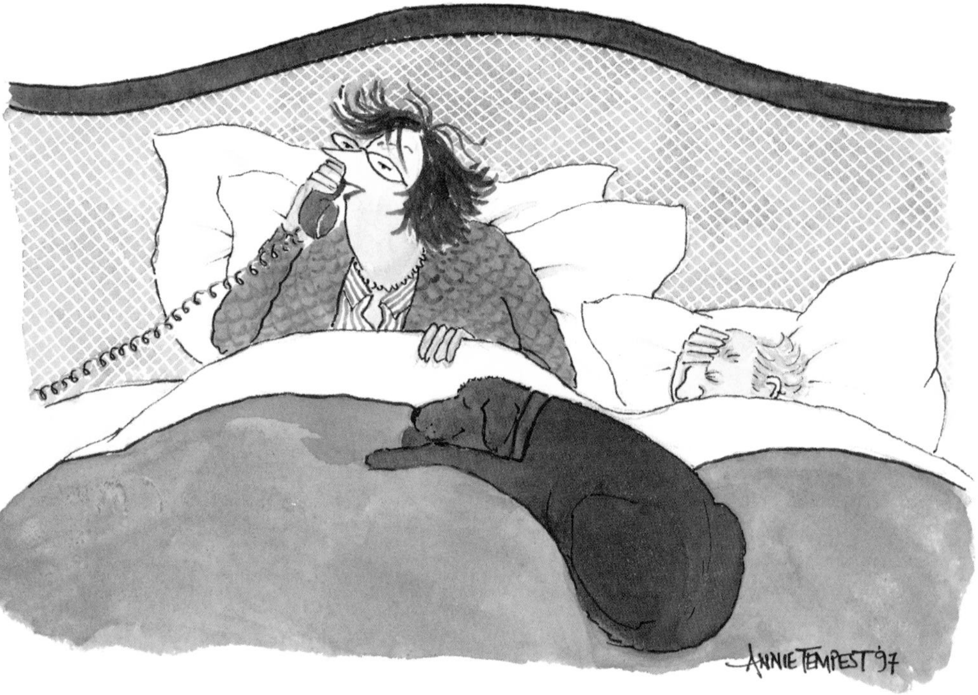
ANNIE TEMPEST '97

" Emergency services? Two large Bloody Marys, please..."

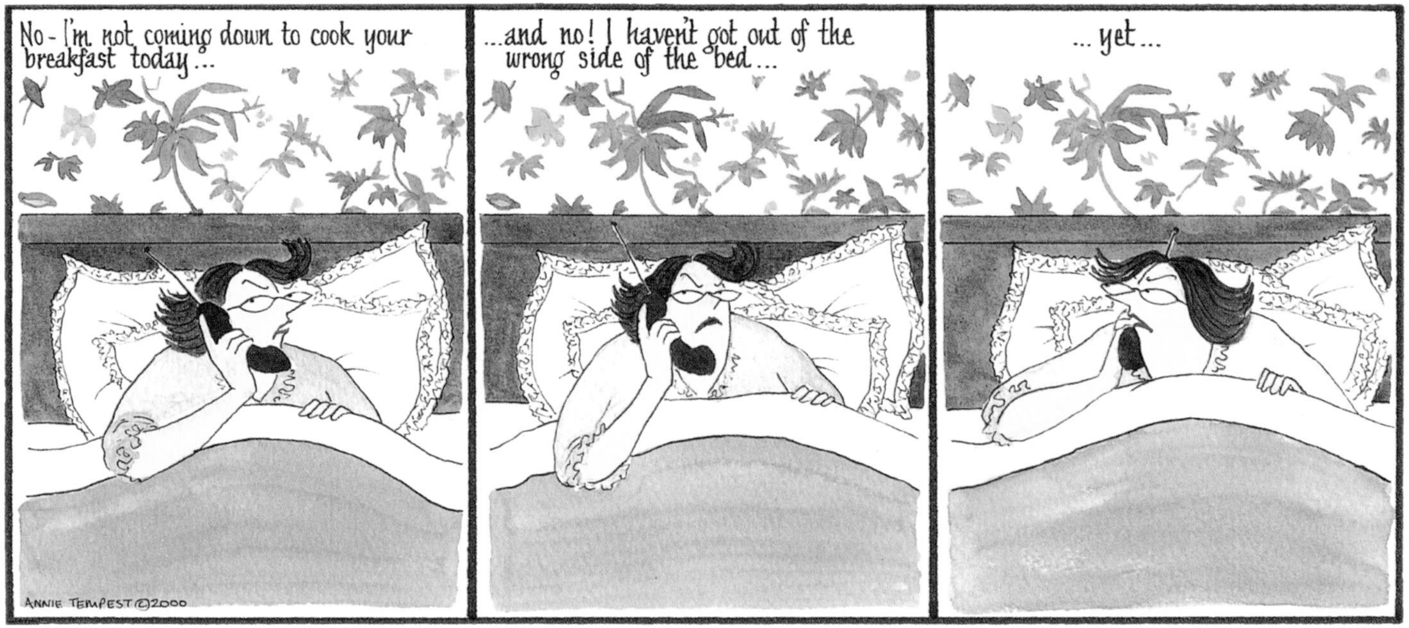
No - I'm not coming down to cook your breakfast today...
...and no! I haven't got out of the wrong side of the bed...
...yet...
ANNIE TEMPEST ©2000

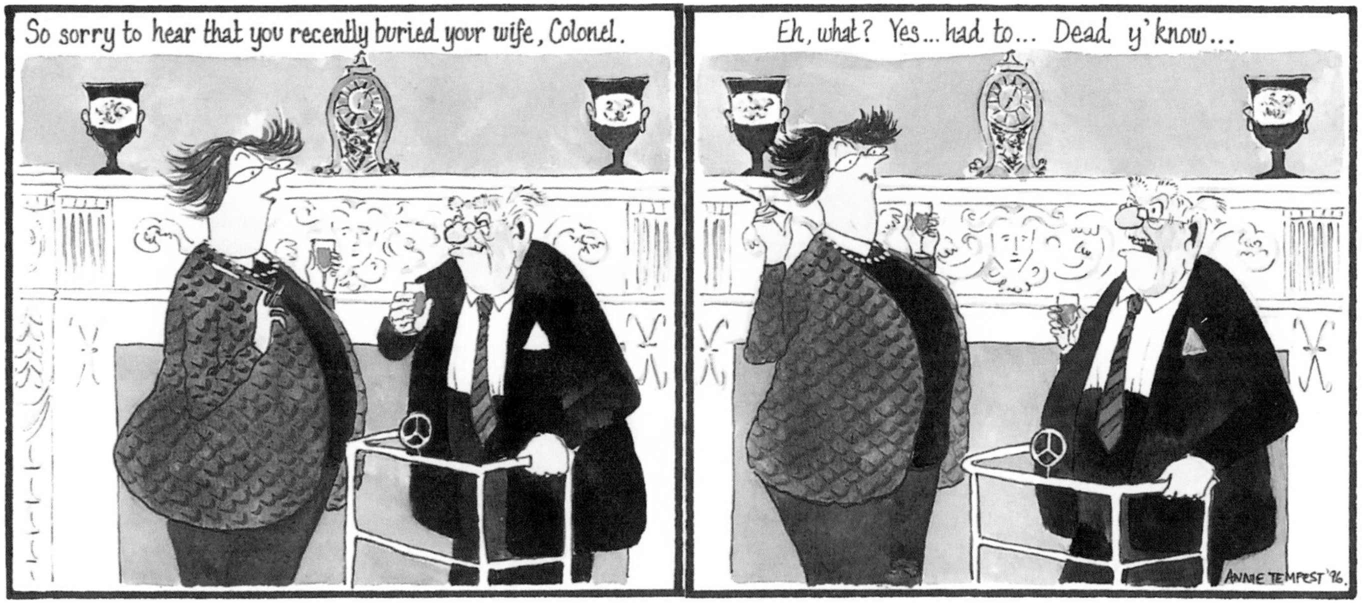
So sorry to hear that you recently buried your wife, Colonel.
Eh, what? Yes... had to... Dead y'know...
ANNIE TEMPEST '96.

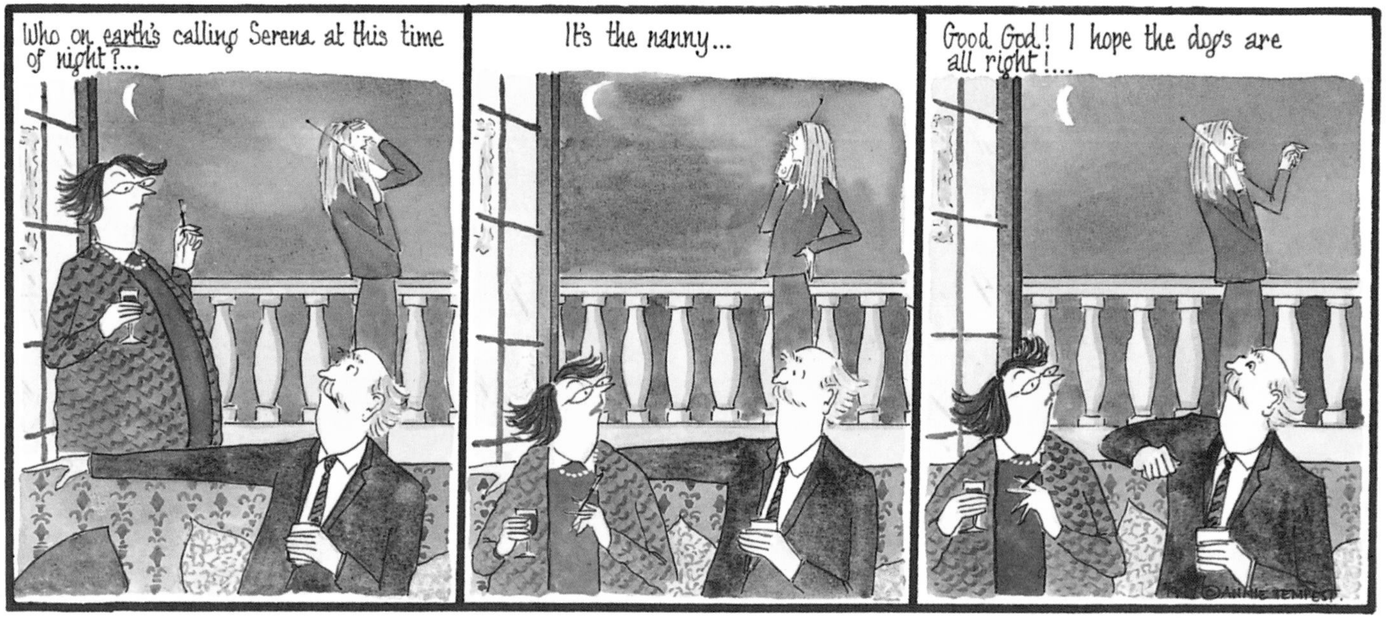
Who on earth's calling Serena at this time of night?...
It's the nanny...
Good God! I hope the dogs are all right!...
©ANNIE TEMPEST.

"If you're hoping for a hot bath, you'll have to catch the boiler unawares at about four o'clock in the morning..."

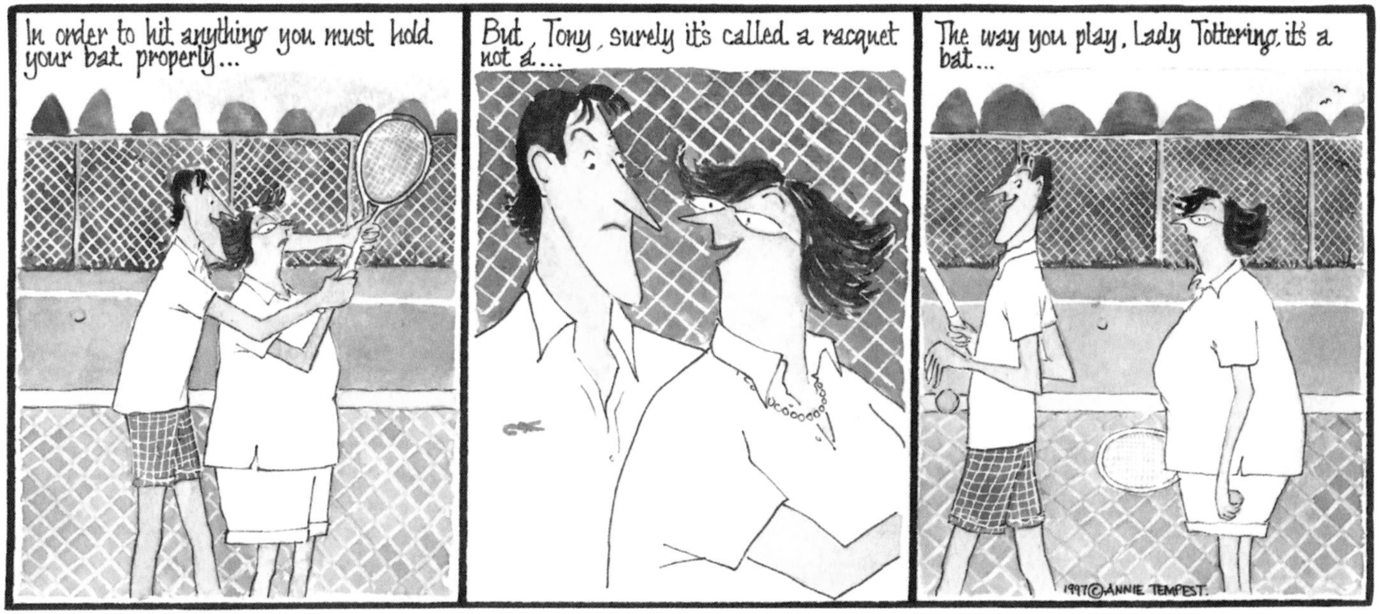
In order to hit anything you must hold your bat properly...
But, Tony, surely it's called a racquet not a....
The way you play, Lady Tottering, it's a bat...
1997 © ANNIE TEMPEST.

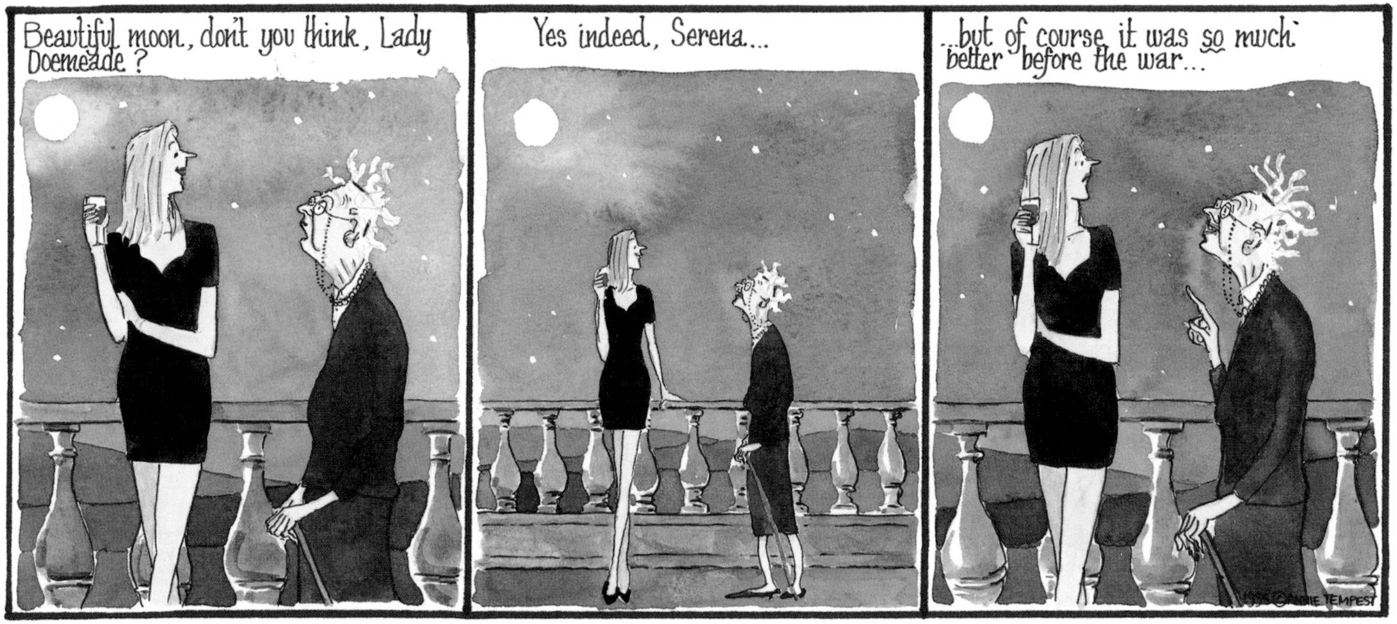
Beautiful moon, don't you think, Lady Doemeade?
Yes indeed, Serena...
...but of course it was so much better before the war...
TEMPEST

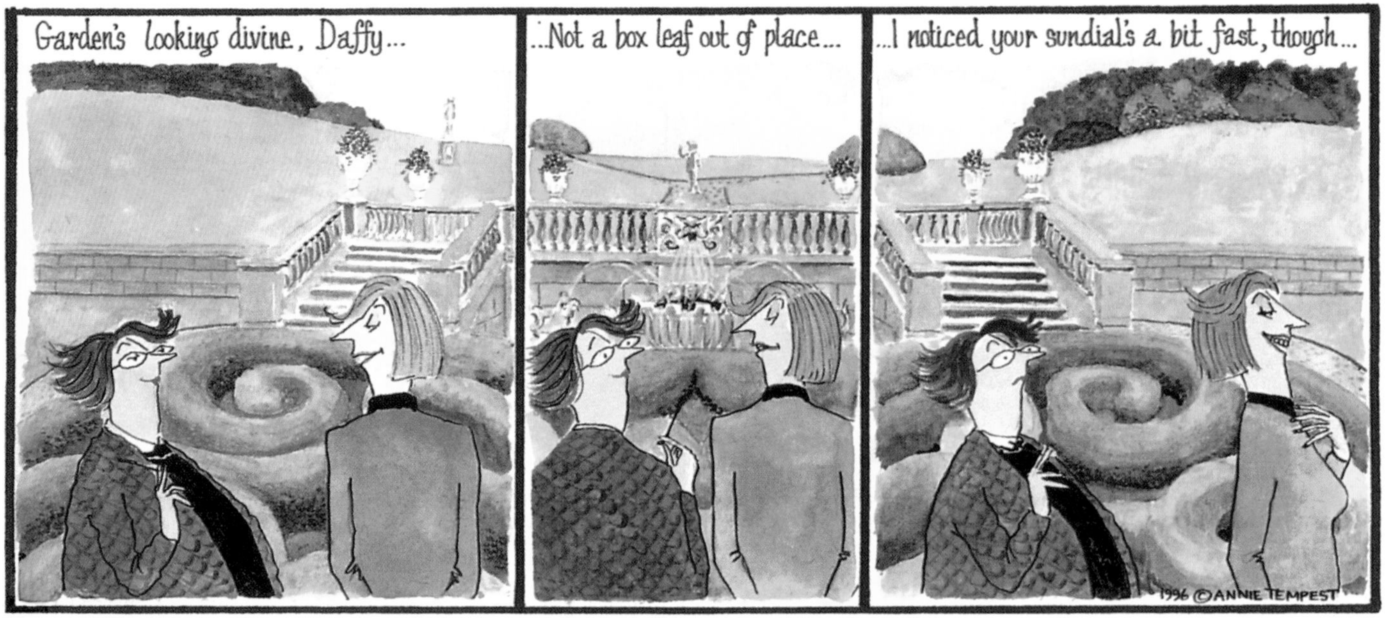
Garden's looking divine, Daffy...
...Not a box leaf out of place...
...I noticed your sundial's a bit fast, though...
1996 © ANNIE TEMPEST

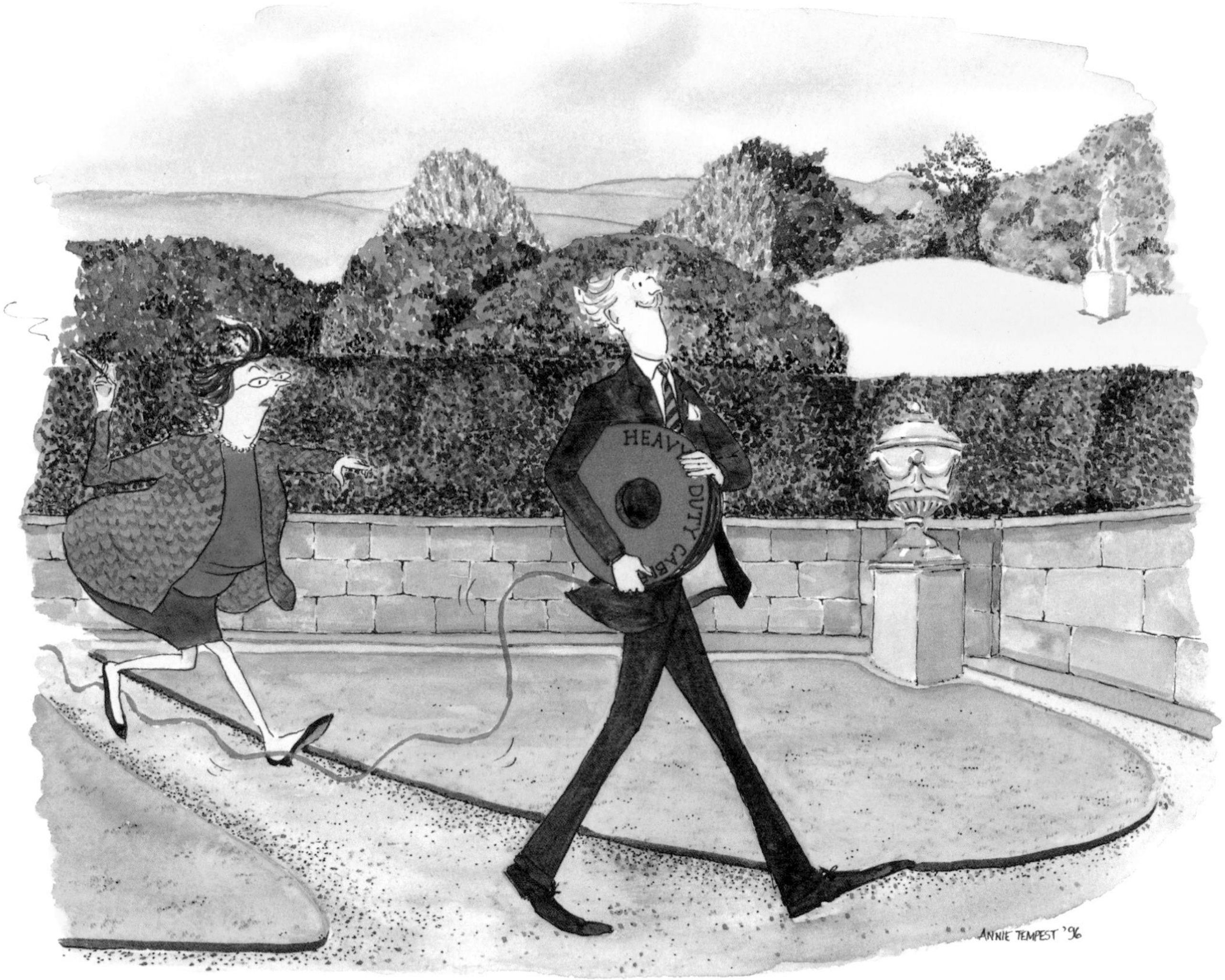
HEAVY DUTY CABLE
ANNIE TEMPEST '96

"...but Dicky won't 500 volts through the urns actually *KILL* the burglars?..."

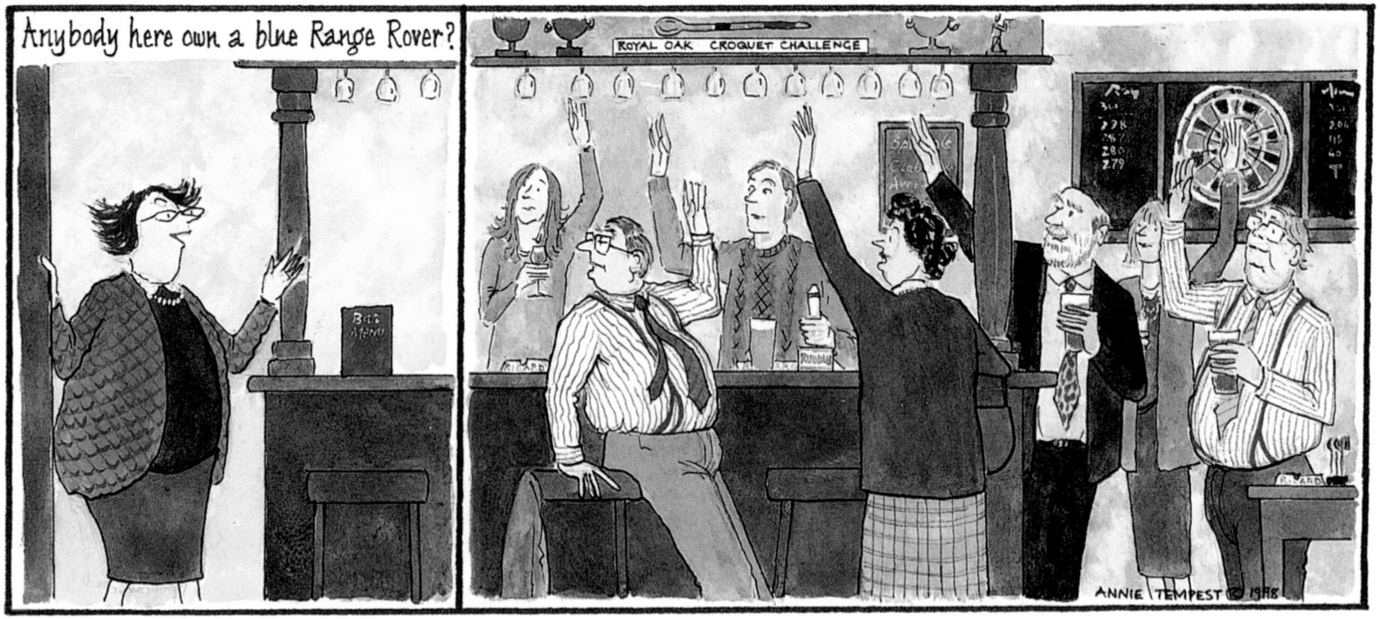
Anybody here own a blue Range Rover?
ROYAL OAK CROQUET CHALLENGE
ANNIE TEMPEST © 1998

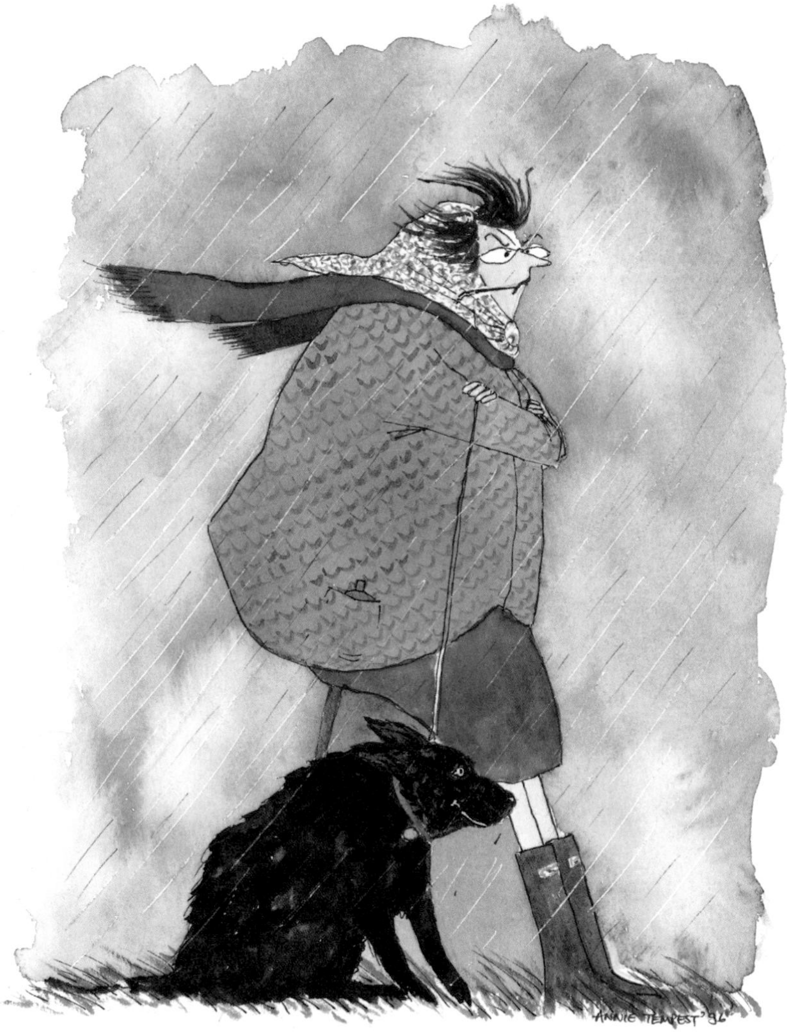
ANNIE TEMPEST '96

Enjoying one's husband's hobbies...

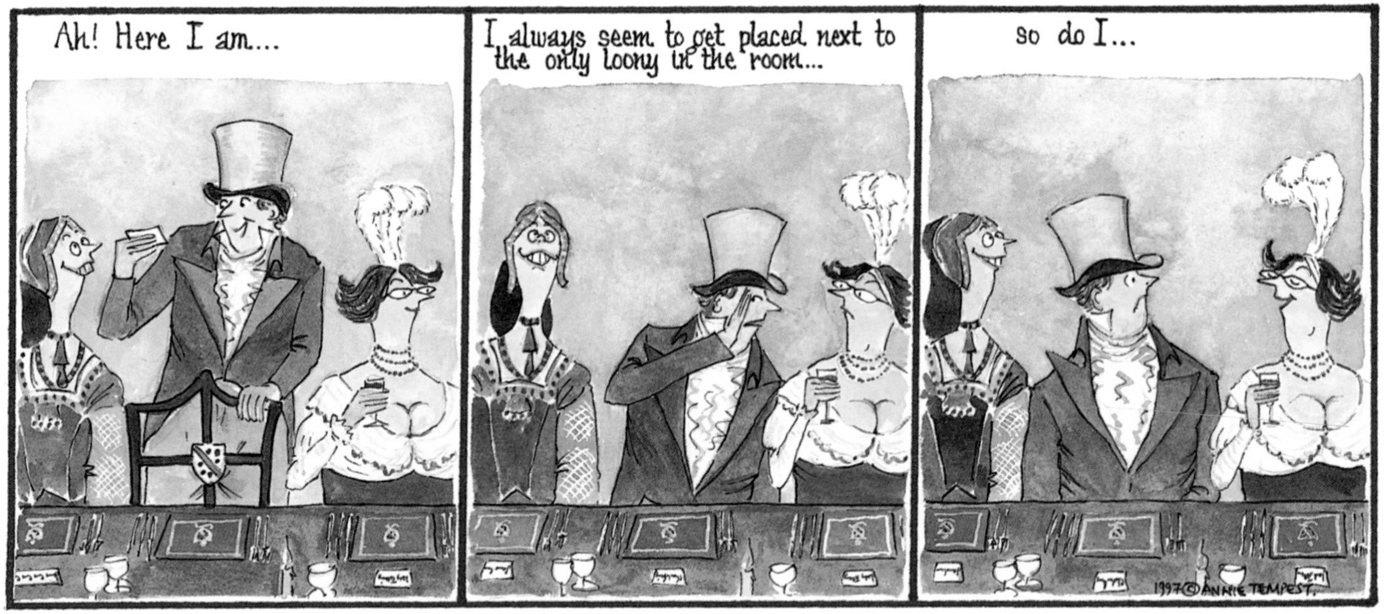
Ah! Here I am....
I always seem to get placed next to the only loony in the room...
so do I...
1997 © ANNIE TEMPEST.

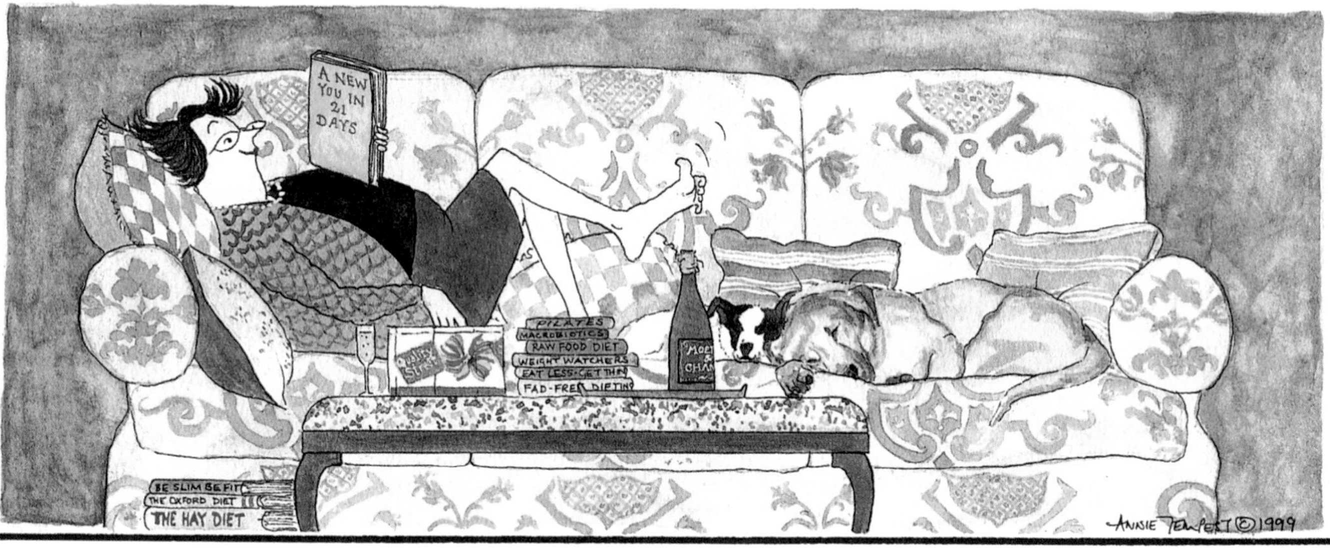
A NEW YOU IN 21 DAYS
PILATES
MACROBIOTICS
RAW FOOD DIET
WEIGHT WATCHERS
BE SLIM BE FIT
THE OXFORD DIET
THE HAY DIET
ANNIE TEMPEST © 1999

Another evening researching the *ONE* diet that's going to work this time...

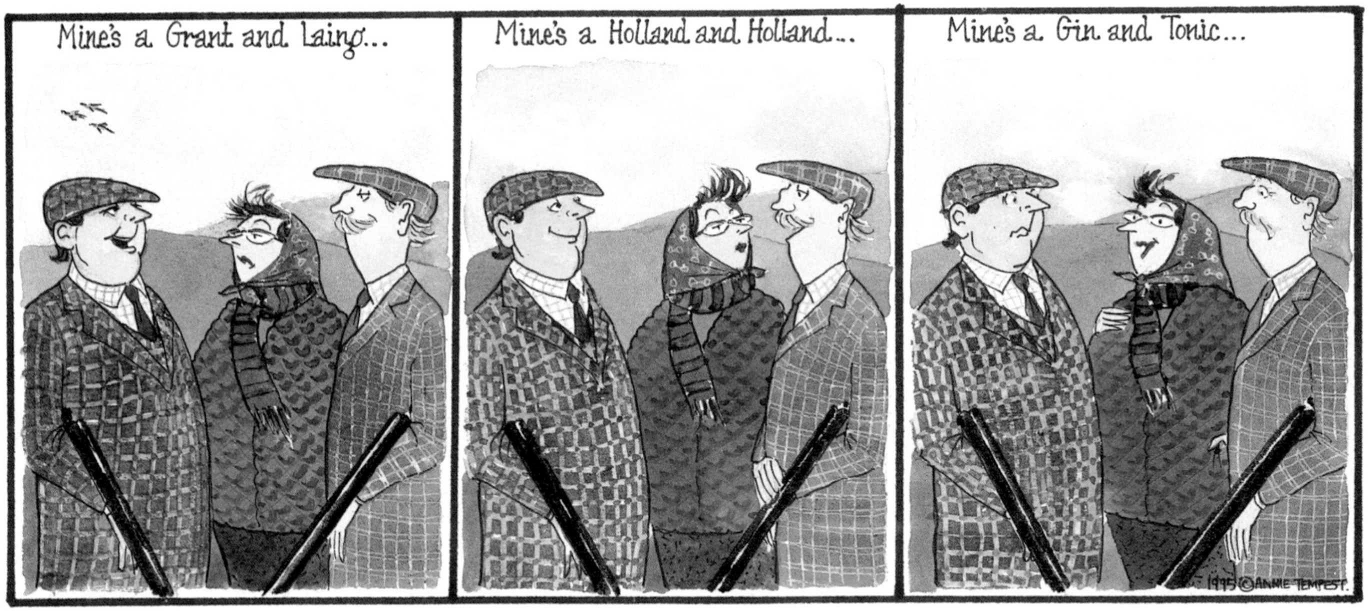
Mine's a Grant and Laing...
Mine's a Holland and Holland...
Mine's a Gin and Tonic...
1995 © ANNIE TEMPEST.

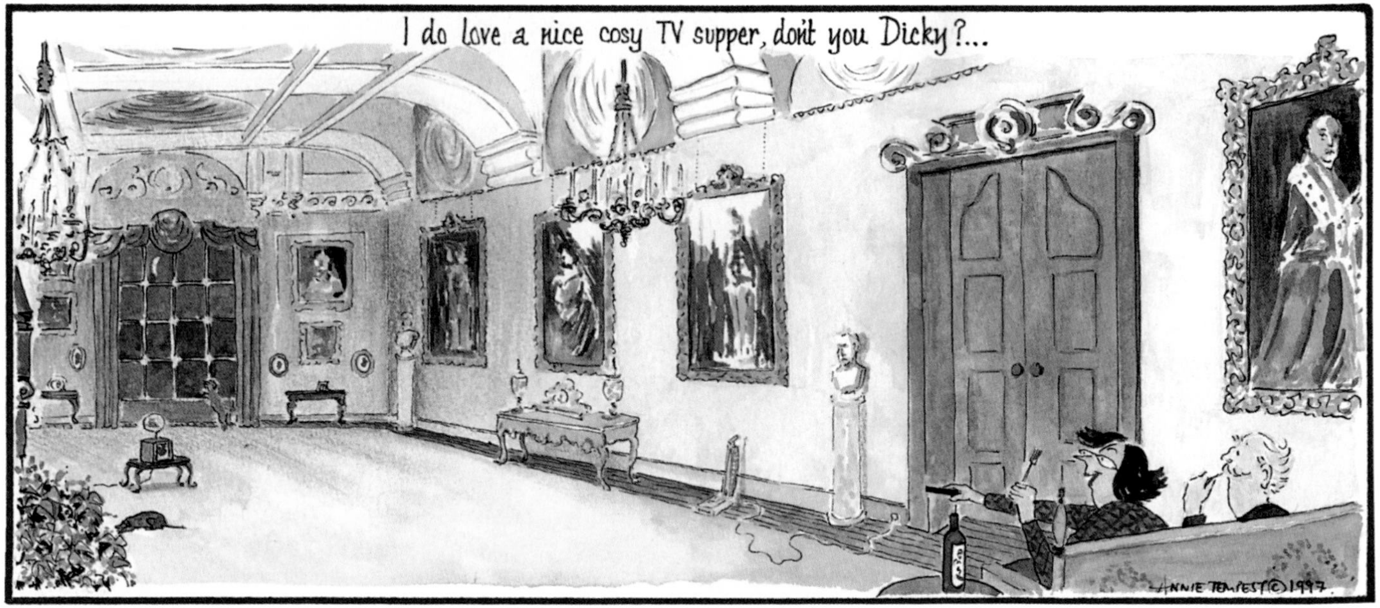
I do love a nice cosy TV supper, don't you Dicky?...
ANNIE TEMPEST © 1997.

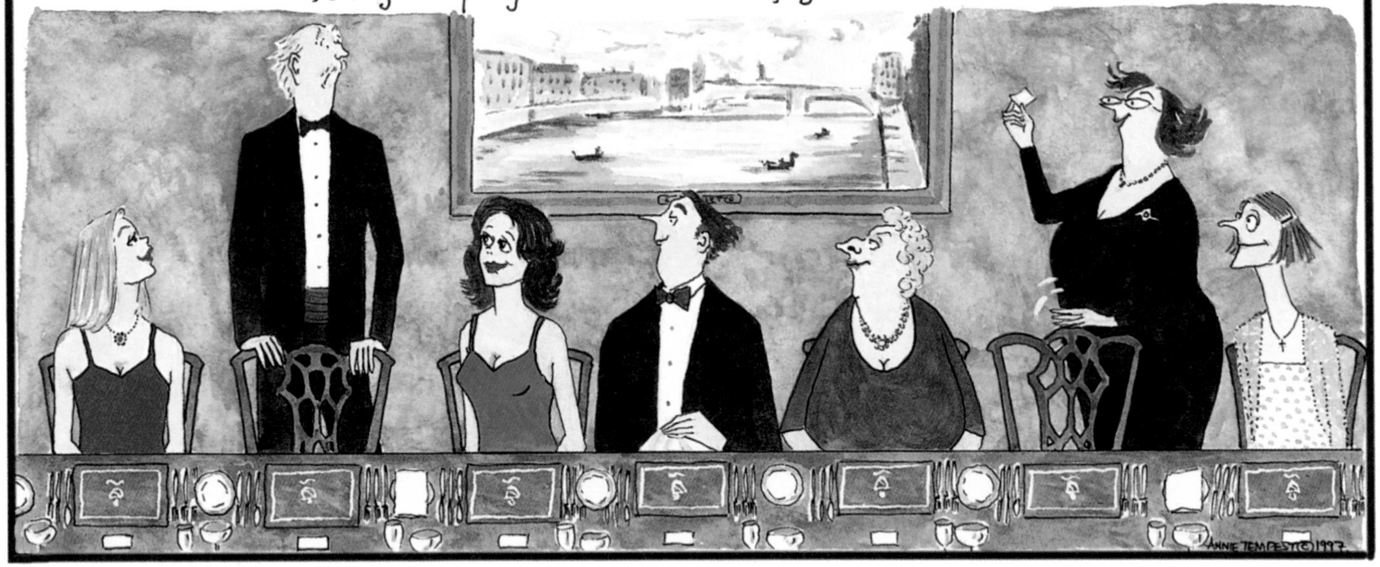
ANNIE TEMPEST © 1997

No, Dicky - I've put you over here between Grizelda and Jane...

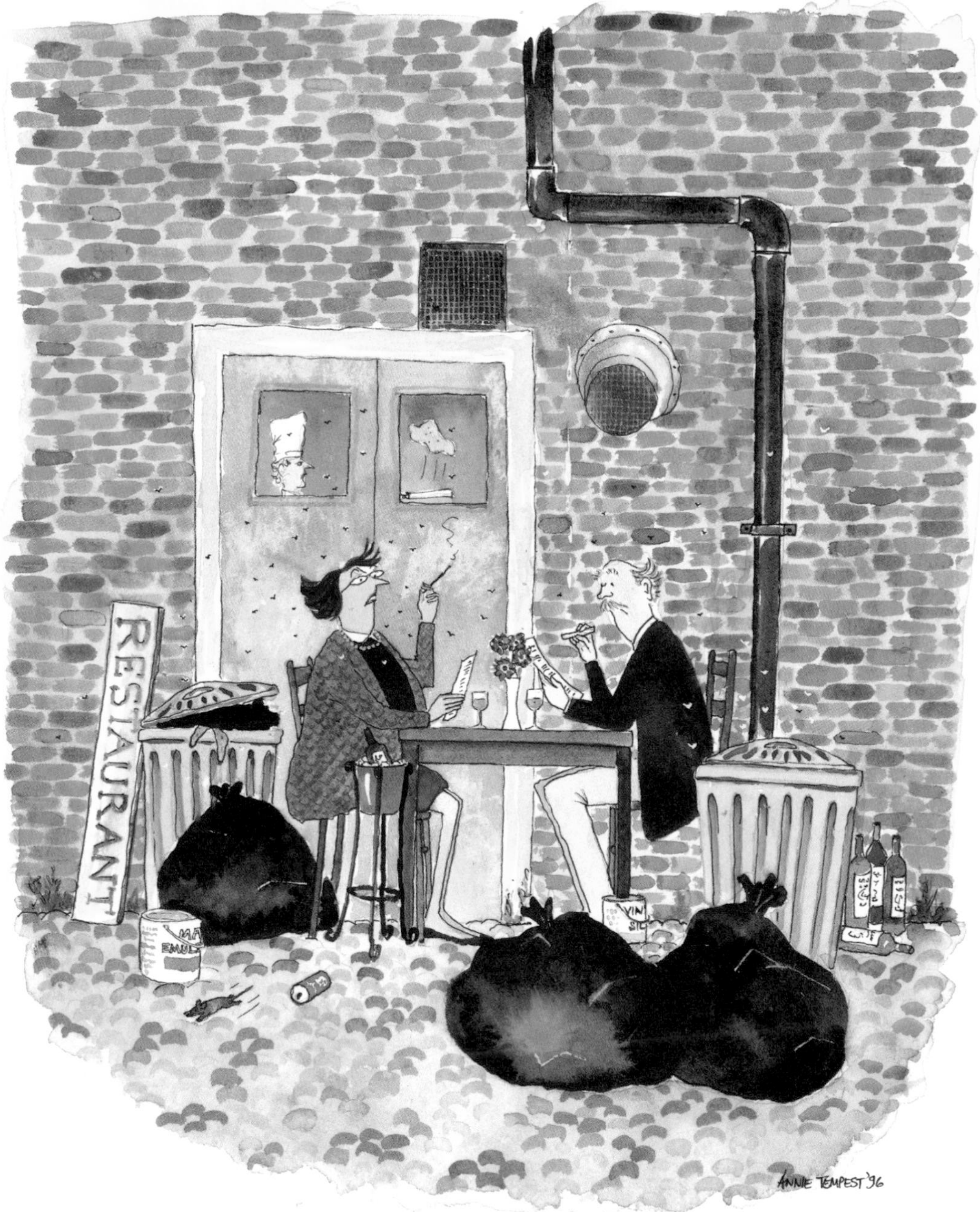
RESTAURANT
ANNIE TEMPEST '96

"Apparently this is the smoking area..."

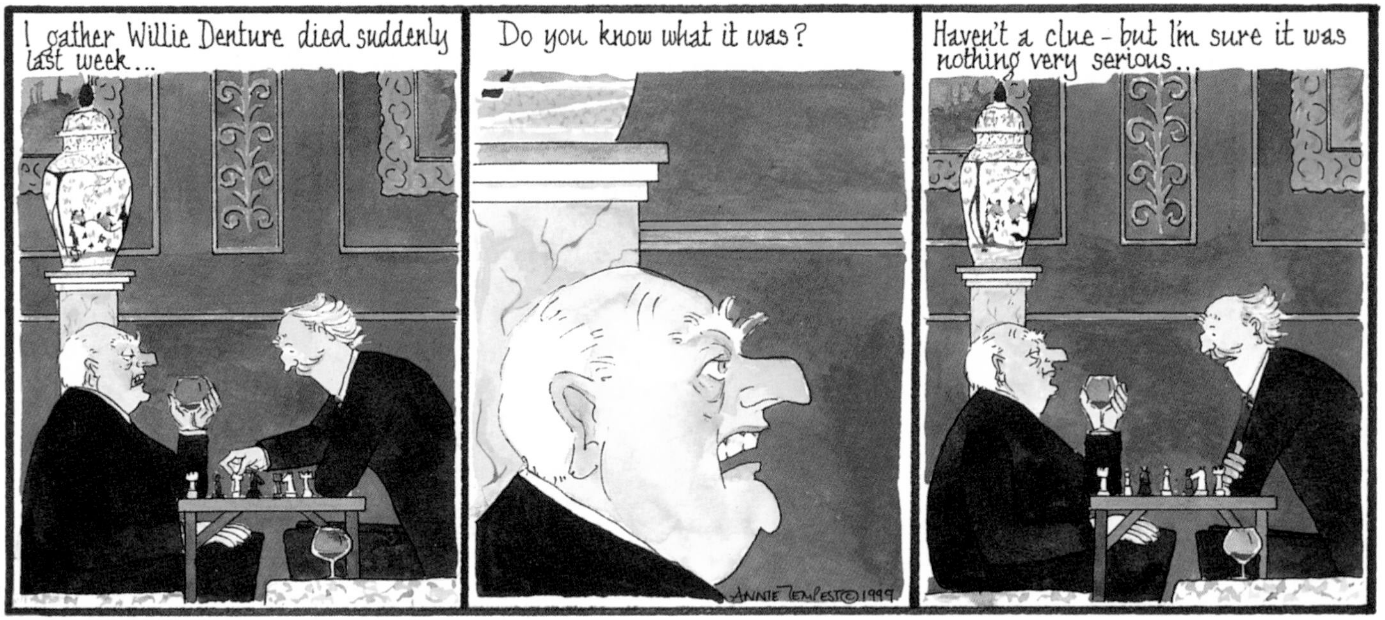
I gather Willie Denture died suddenly last week...
Do you know what it was?
ANNIE TEMPEST © 1999
Haven't a clue - but I'm sure it was nothing very serious...

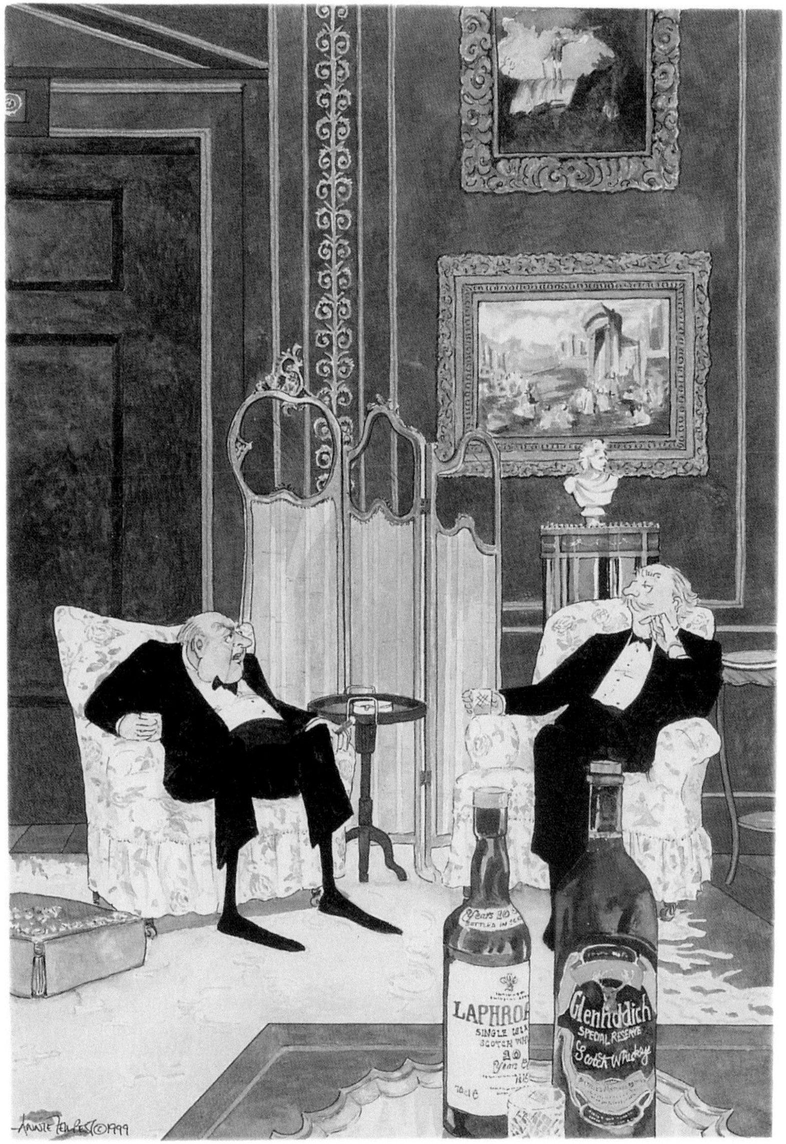
LAPHROA
SINGLE ISLA
Glenfiddich
SPECIAL RESERVE
Scotch Whisky

"... The future's not what it used to be, Dicky..."

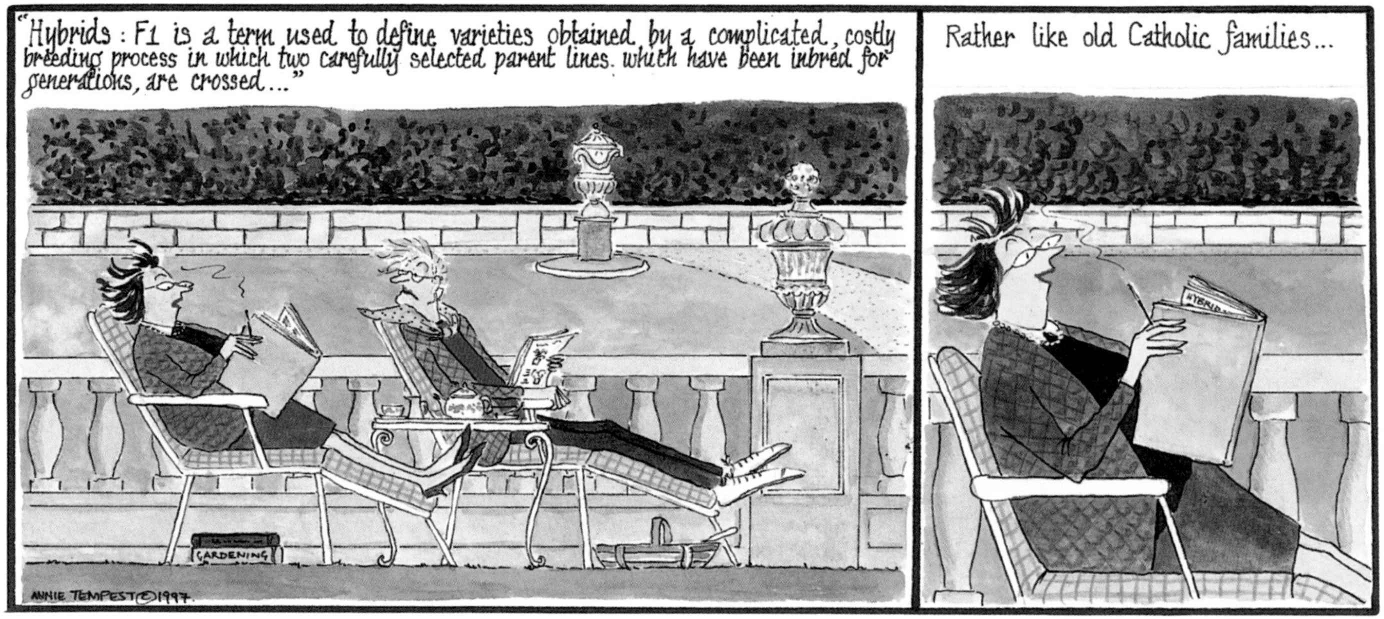
"Hybrids: F1 is a term used to define varieties obtained by a complicated, costly breeding process in which two carefully selected parent lines. which have been inbred for generations, are crossed..."
GARDENING
ANNIE TEMPEST © 1997.
Rather like old Catholic families...

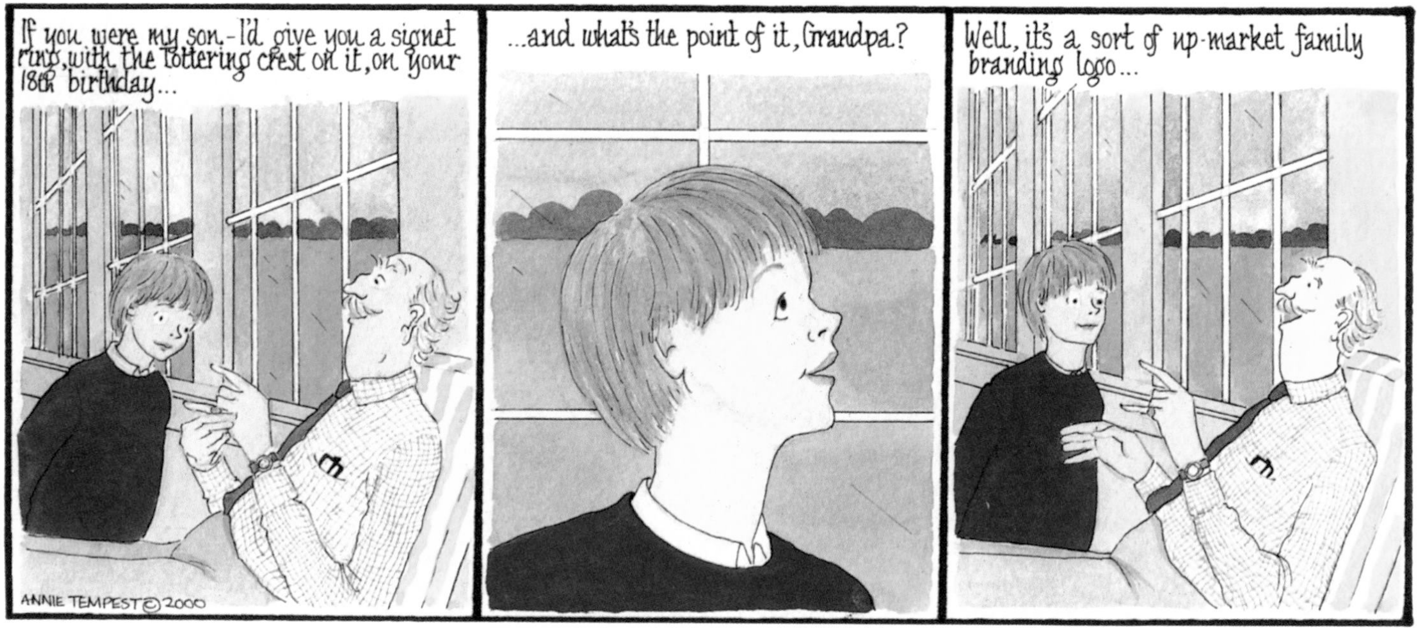
If you were my son - I'd give you a signet ring, with the Tottering crest on it, on your 18th birthday...
ANNIE TEMPEST © 2000
...and what's the point of it, Grandpa?
Well, it's a sort of up-market family branding logo...

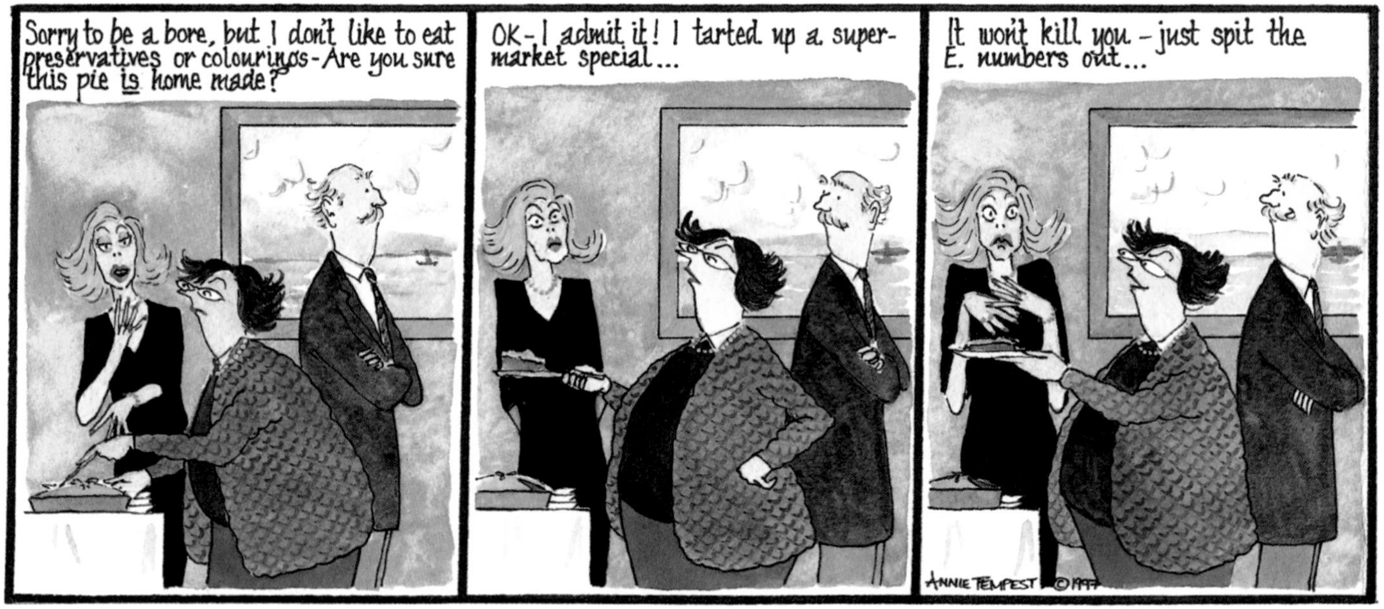
Sorry to be a bore, but I don't like to eat preservatives or colourings - Are you sure this pie is home made?
OK - I admit it! I tarted up a super-market special...
It won't kill you - just spit the E. numbers out...
ANNIE TEMPEST ©1997

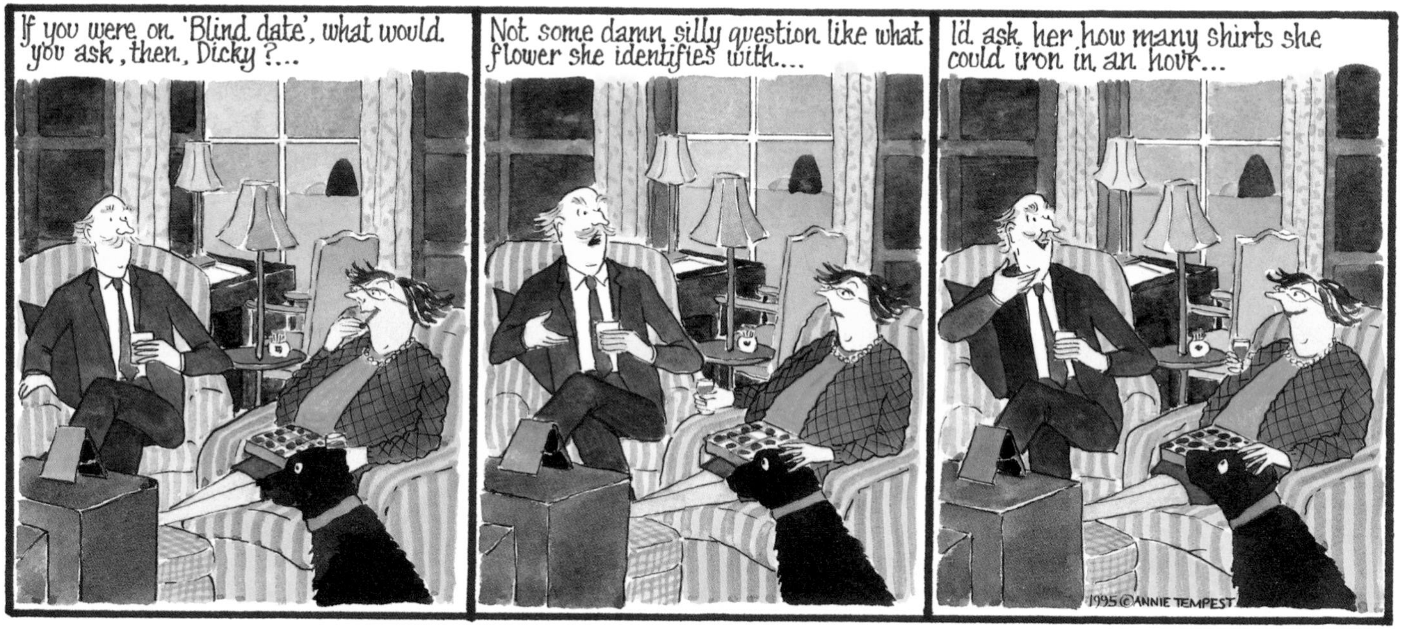
If you were on 'Blind date', what would you ask, then, Dicky?...
Not some damn silly question like what flower she identifies with....
I'd ask her how many shirts she could iron in an hour...
1995 © ANNIE TEMPEST

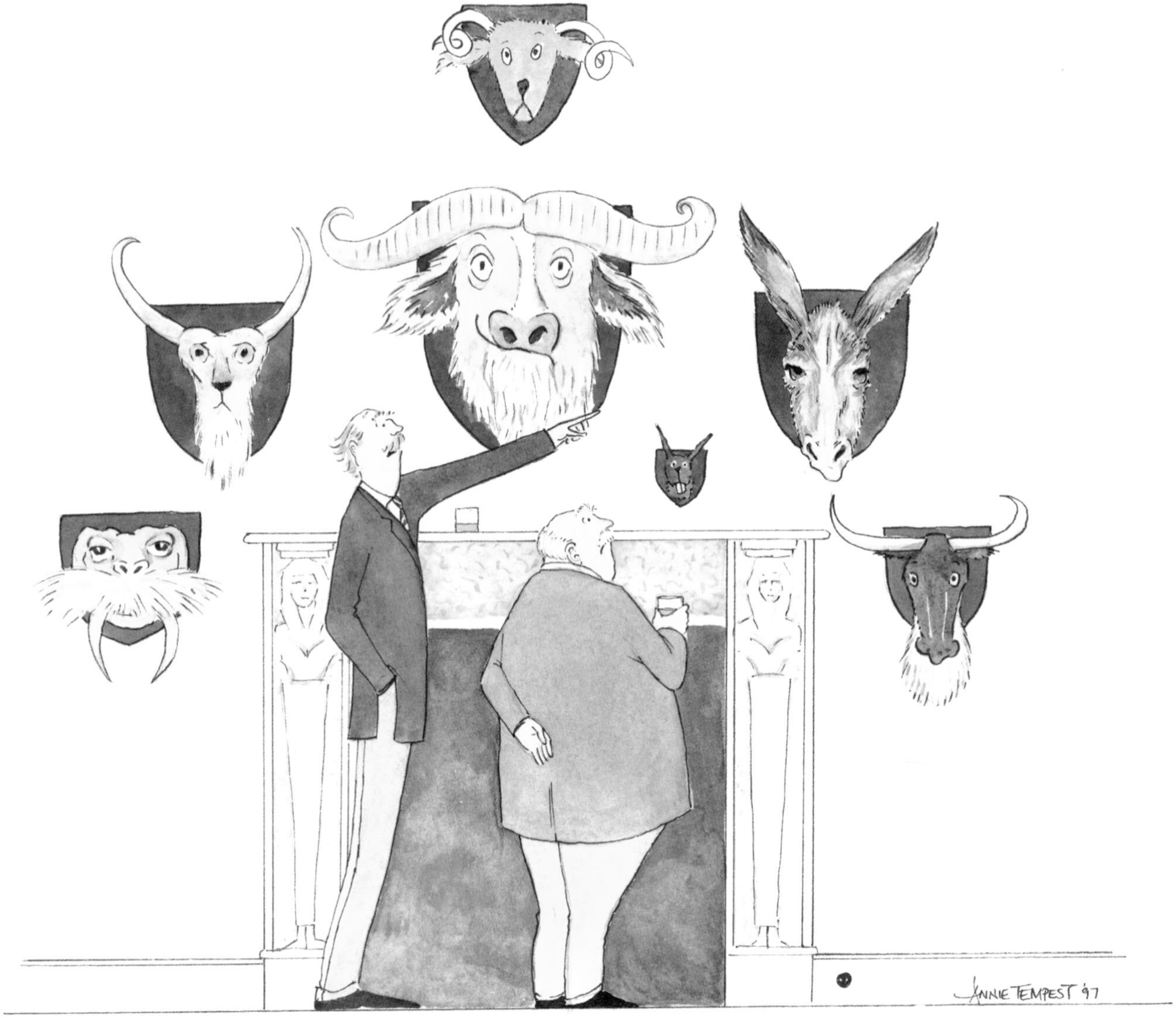
ANNIE TEMPEST '97

"One of my wife's friends talked the hind legs off that one..."

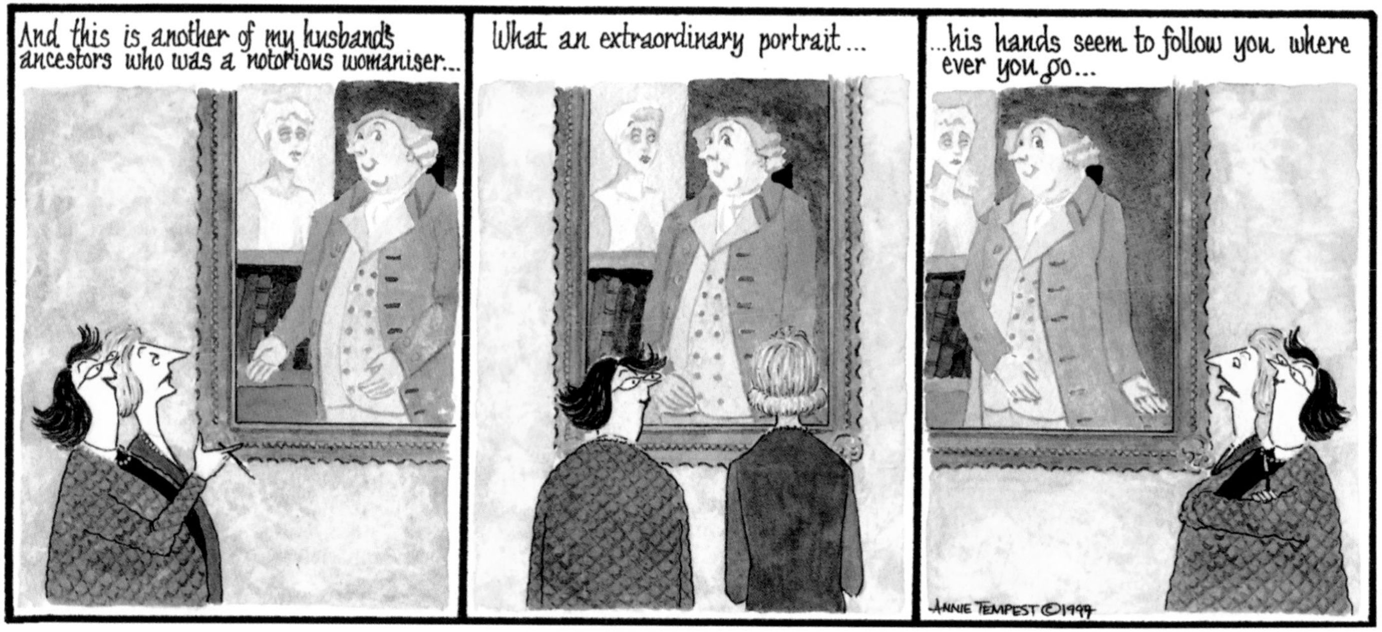
And this is another of my husband's ancestors who was a notorious womaniser...
What an extraordinary portrait...
...his hands seem to follow you where ever you go...
ANNIE TEMPEST ©1997

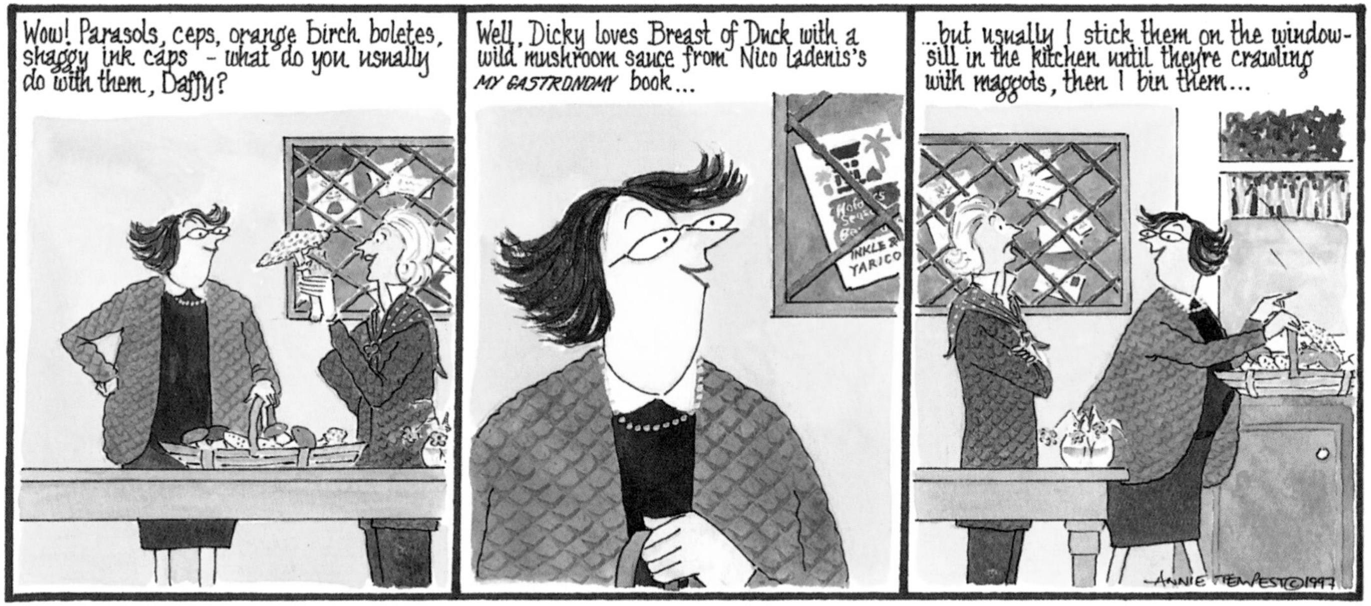
Wow! Parasols, ceps, orange birch boletes, shaggy ink caps - what do you usually do with them, Daffy?
Well, Dicky loves Breast of Duck with a wild mushroom sauce from Nico Ladenis's MY GASTRONOMY book...
INKLE & YARICO
...but usually I stick them on the window-sill in the kitchen until they're crawling with maggots, then I bin them...
ANNIE TEMPEST©1997

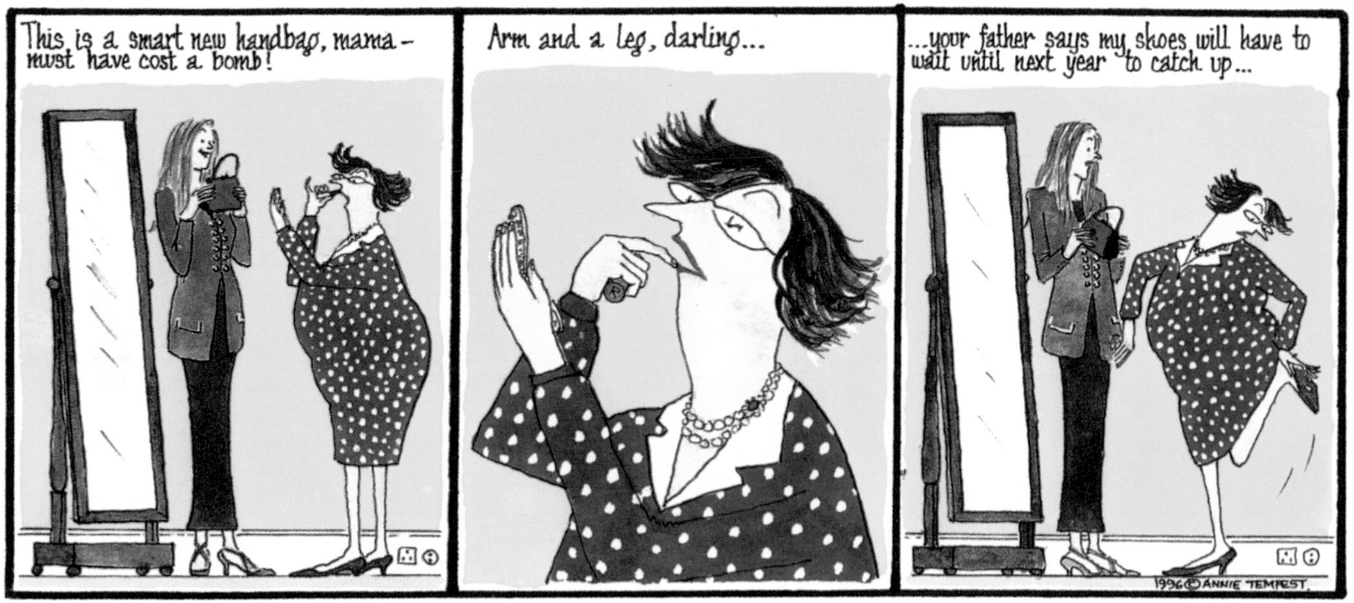
This is a smart new handbag, mama - must have cost a bomb!
Arm and a leg, darling...
...your father says my shoes will have to wait until next year to catch up...
1996 © ANNIE TEMPEST.

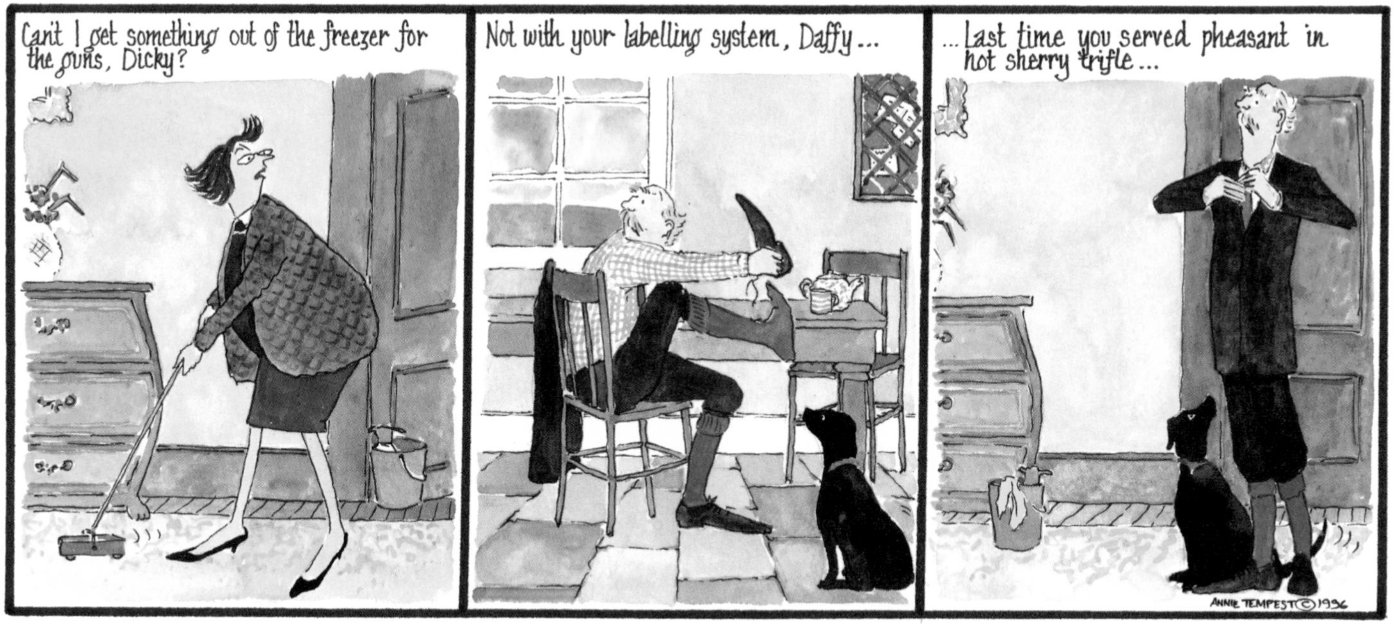
Can't I get something out of the freezer for the guns, Dicky?
Not with your labelling system, Daffy...
...Last time you served pheasant in hot sherry trifle...
ANNIE TEMPEST © 1996

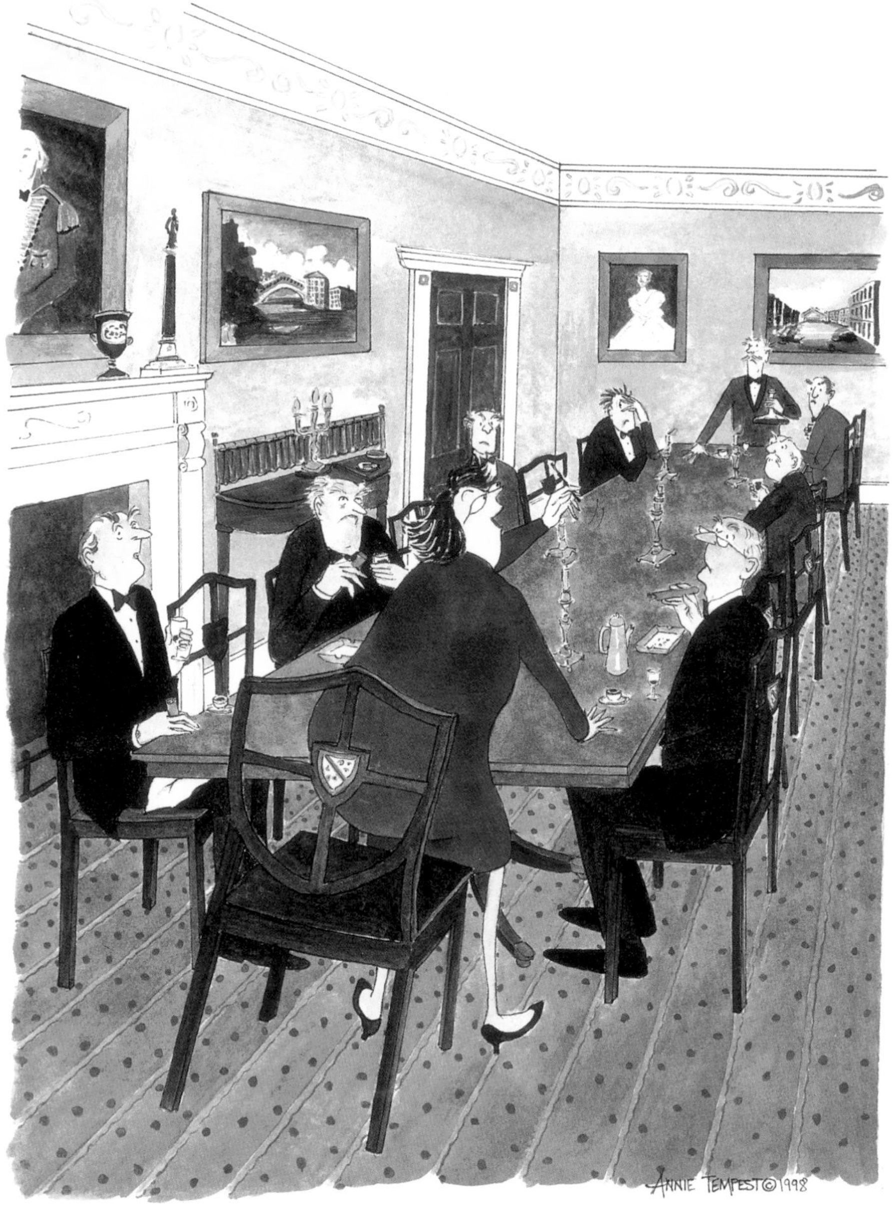
ANNIE TEMPEST © 1998

"To hell with convention! I'm staying and you can pass the port cross-country, Dicky!..."

Imagine if children were like vintage wines, James...

You could store them away in the cellar for twenty years...

...and they'd reach maturity all on their own...

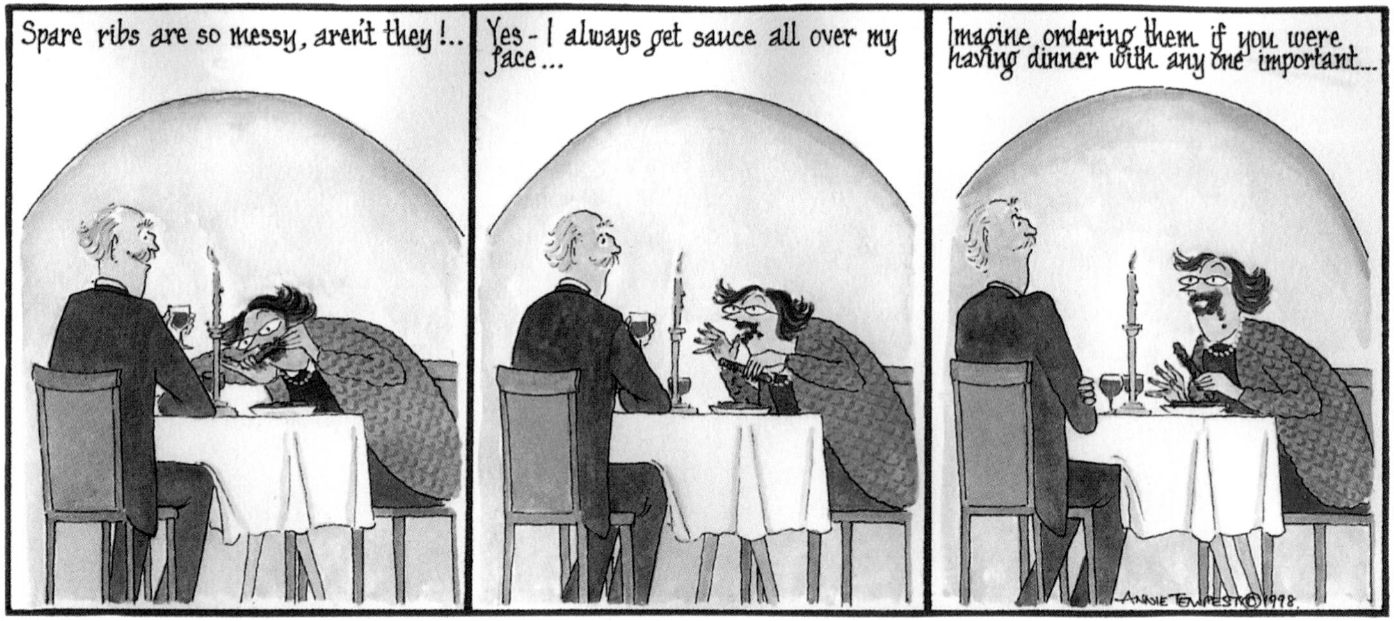
Spare ribs are so messy, aren't they!..
Yes - I always get sauce all over my face...
Imagine ordering them if you were having dinner with any one important...
ANNIE TEMPEST © 1998

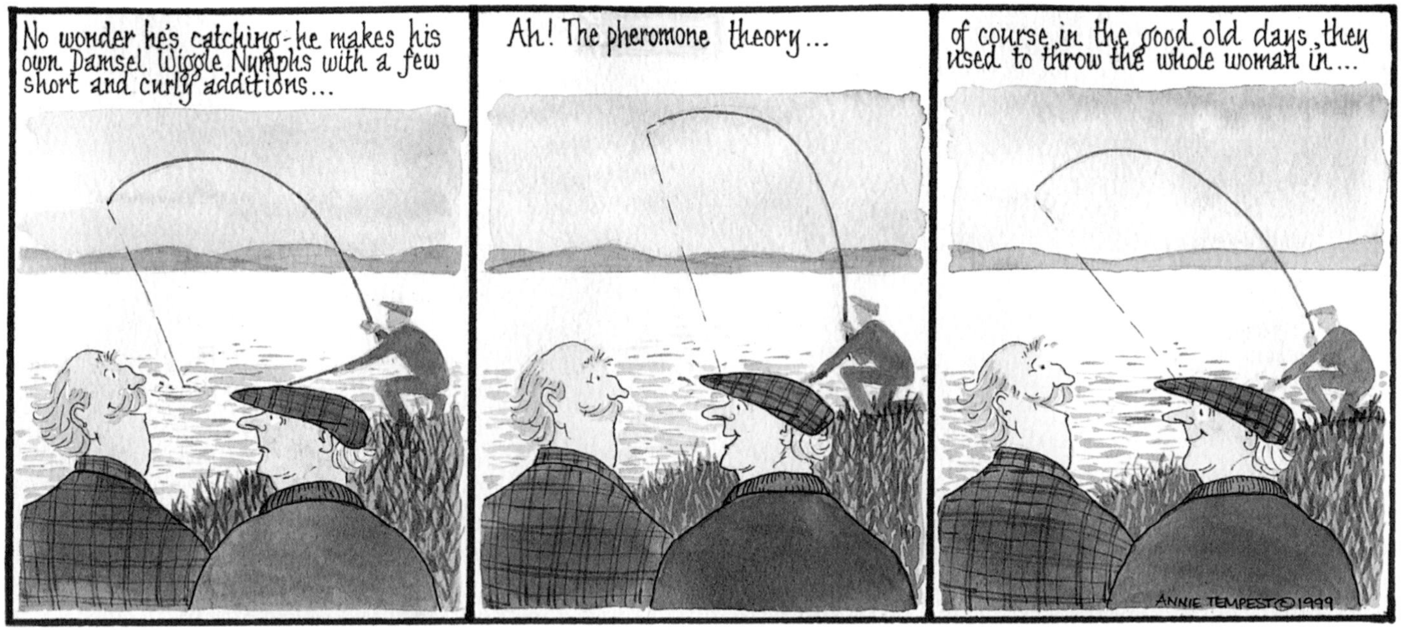
No wonder he's catching - he makes his own Damsel Wiggle Nymphs with a few short and curly additions...
Ah! The pheromone theory...
of course in the good old days, they used to throw the whole woman in...
ANNIE TEMPEST © 1999

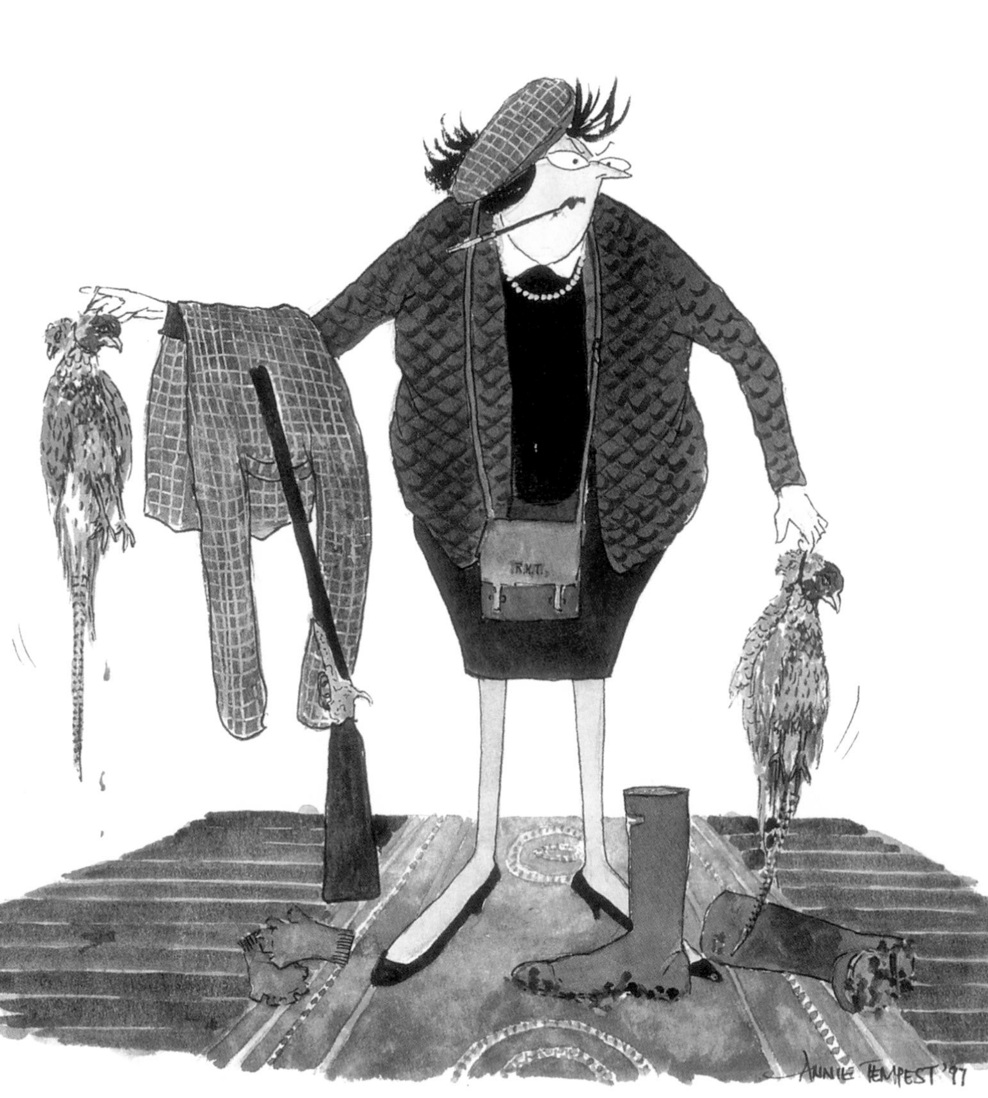
ANNIE TEMPEST '97

The gun who mistook his wife for a servant

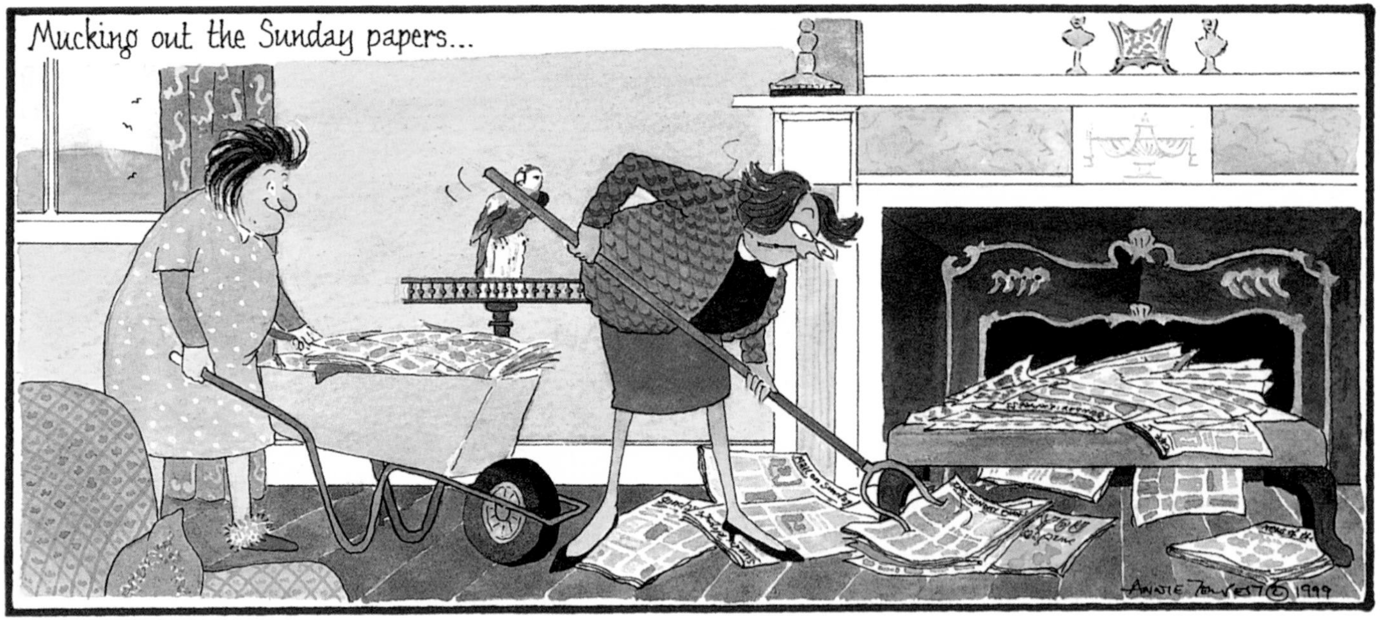
ANNIE TEMPEST © 1999
Mucking out the Sunday papers...

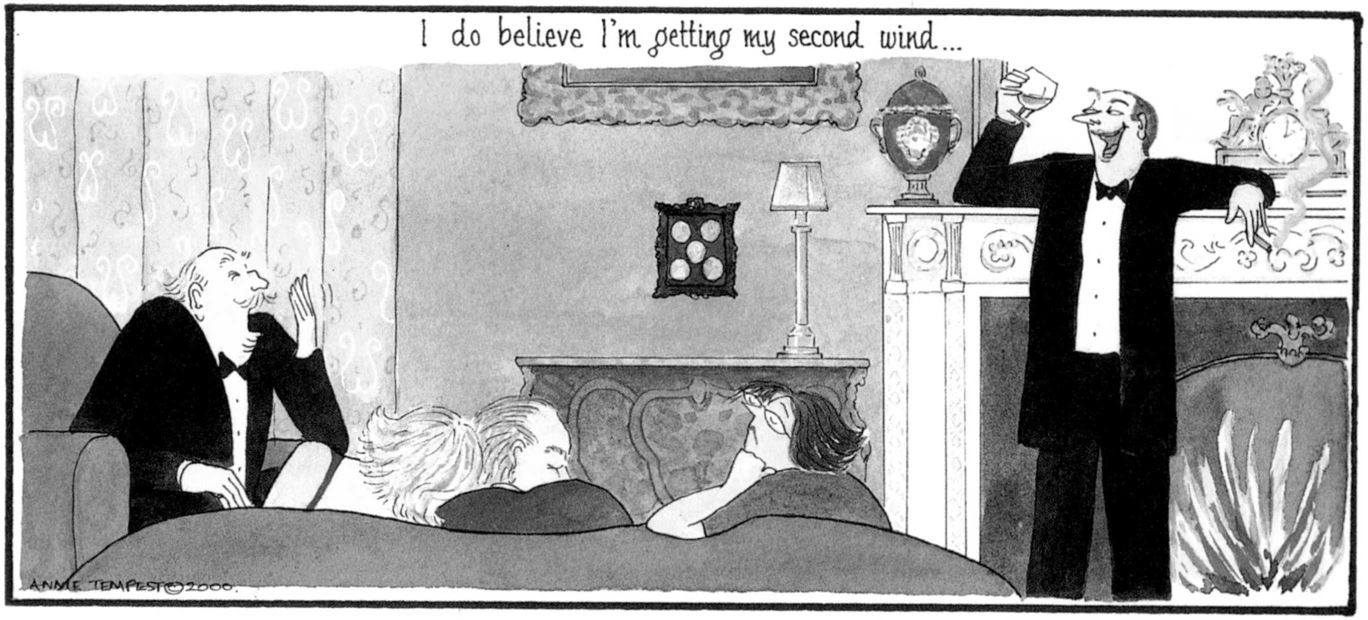
ANNIE TEMPEST © 2000.

I do believe I'm getting my second wind...

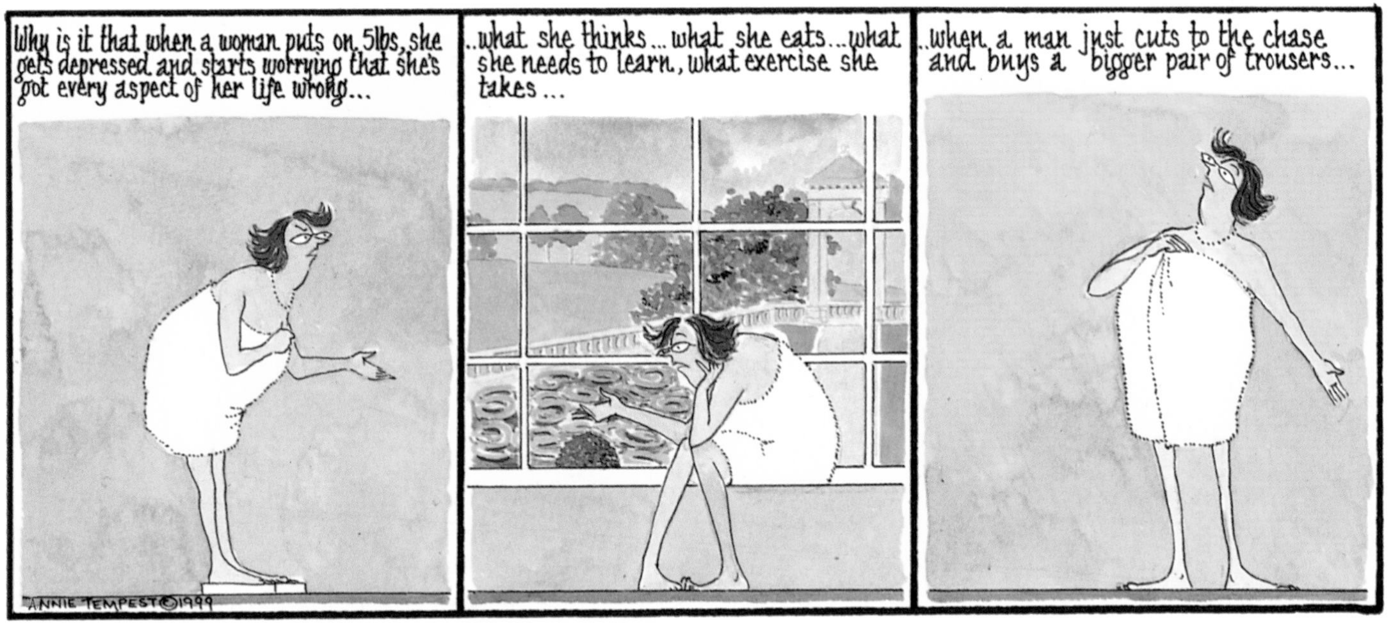
Why is it that when a woman puts on 5lbs, she gets depressed and starts worrying that she's got every aspect of her life wrong...
..what she thinks... what she eats...what she needs to learn, what exercise she takes...
..when a man just cuts to the chase and buys a bigger pair of trousers...
ANNIE TEMPEST © 1999

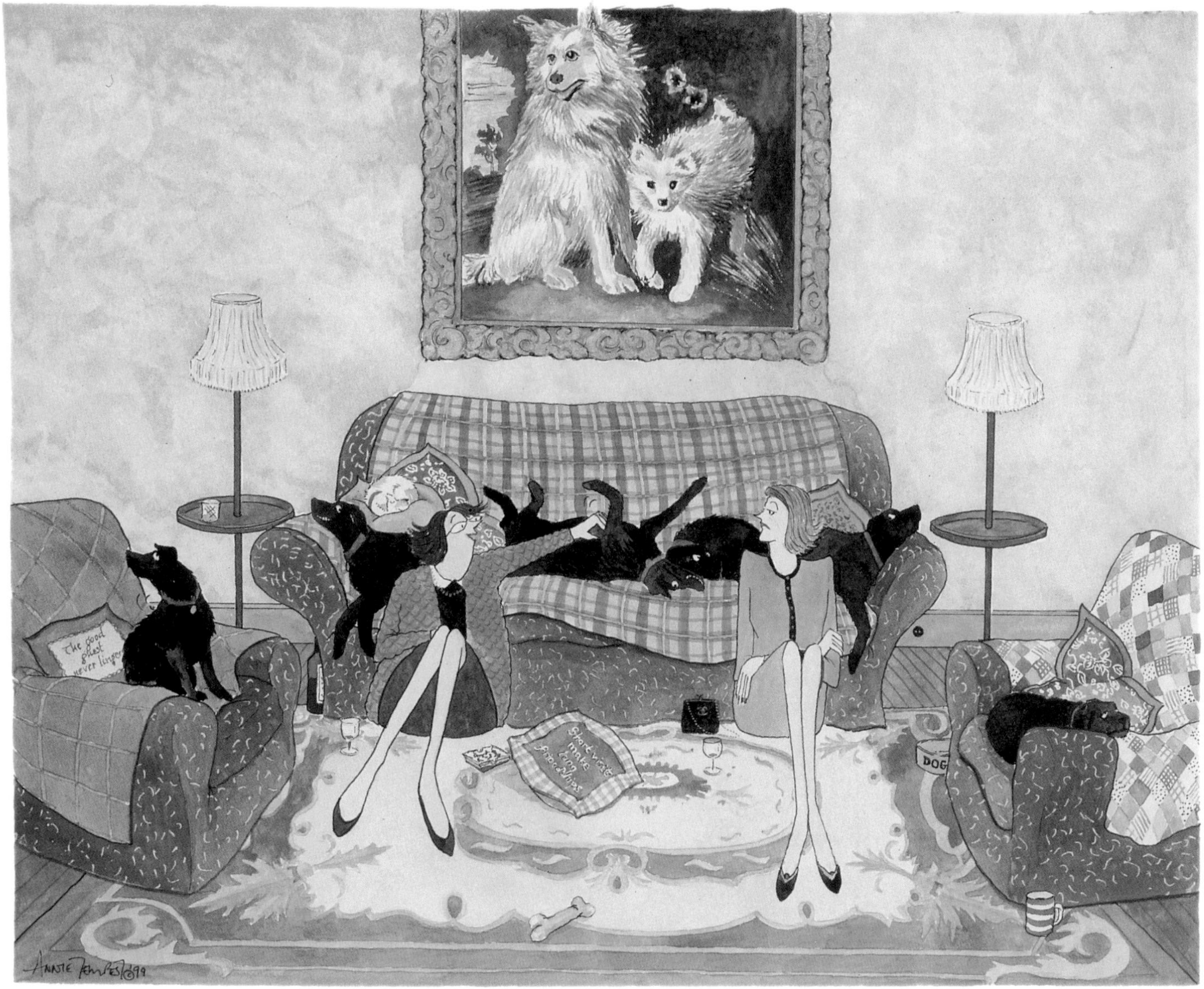
The good guest never linger
Short visits make long friendships
DOG

"... Maybe you'd like a glass of water before you go?..."

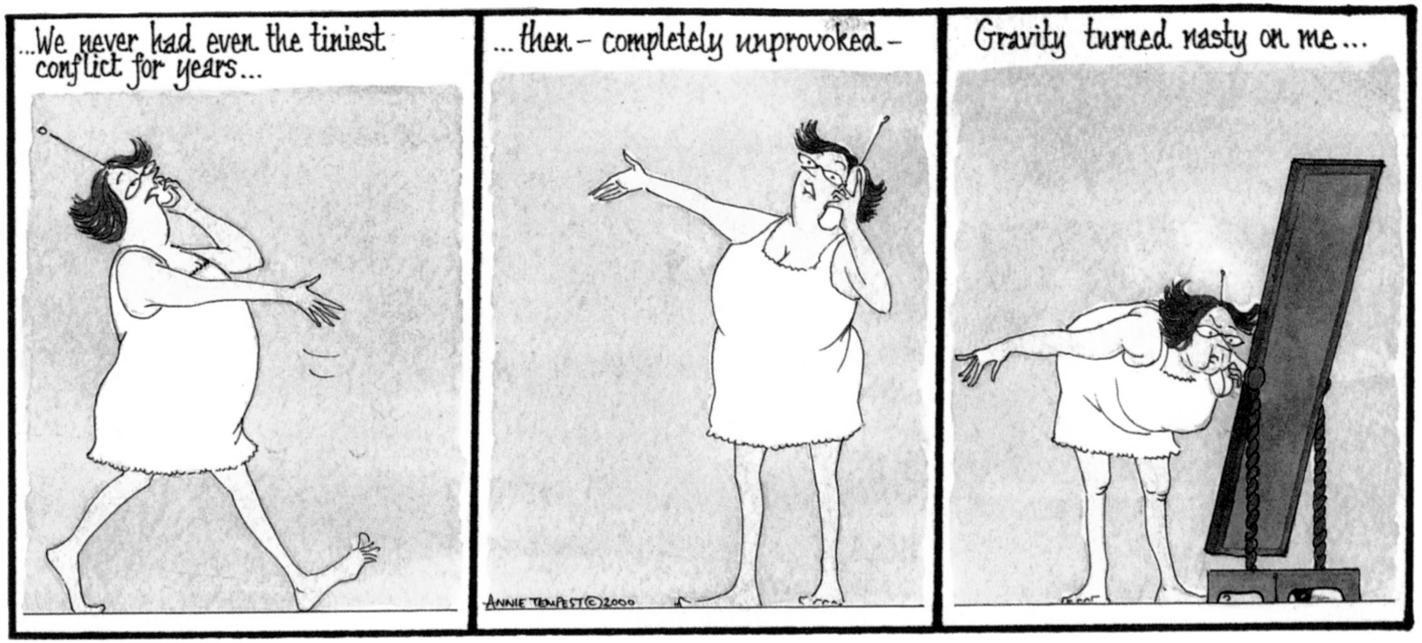
...We never had even the tiniest conflict for years...
...then – completely unprovoked –
Gravity turned nasty on me...
ANNIE TEMPEST © 2000

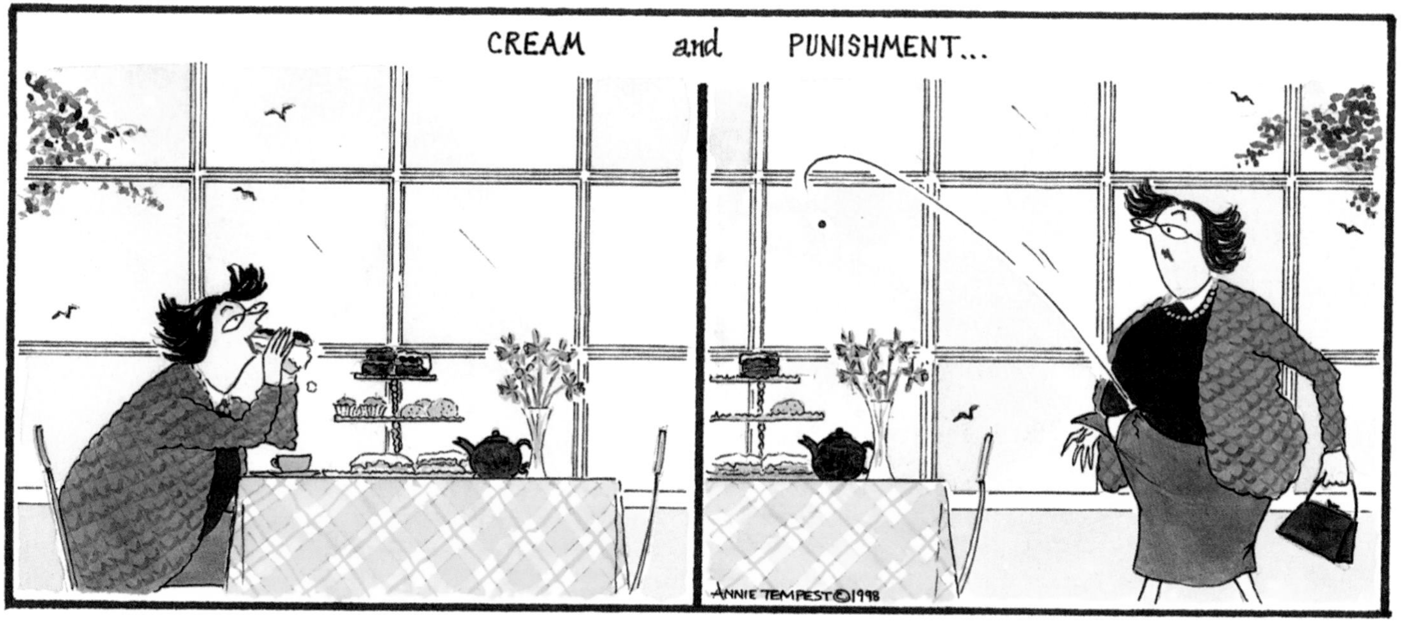
CREAM and PUNISHMENT...
ANNIE TEMPEST © 1998

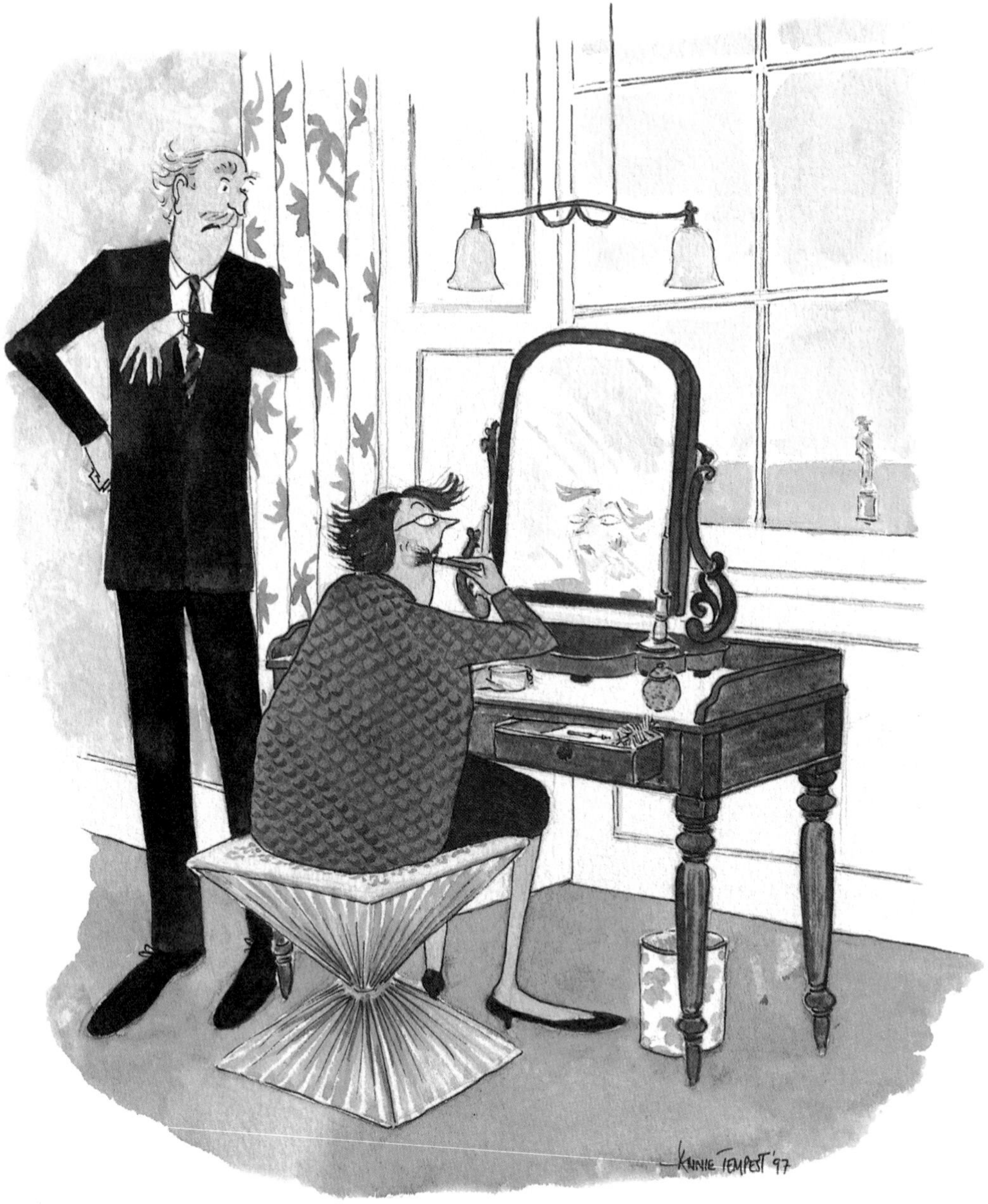
ANNIE TEMPEST '97

"Are you ready yet, or is that just the undercoat?..."

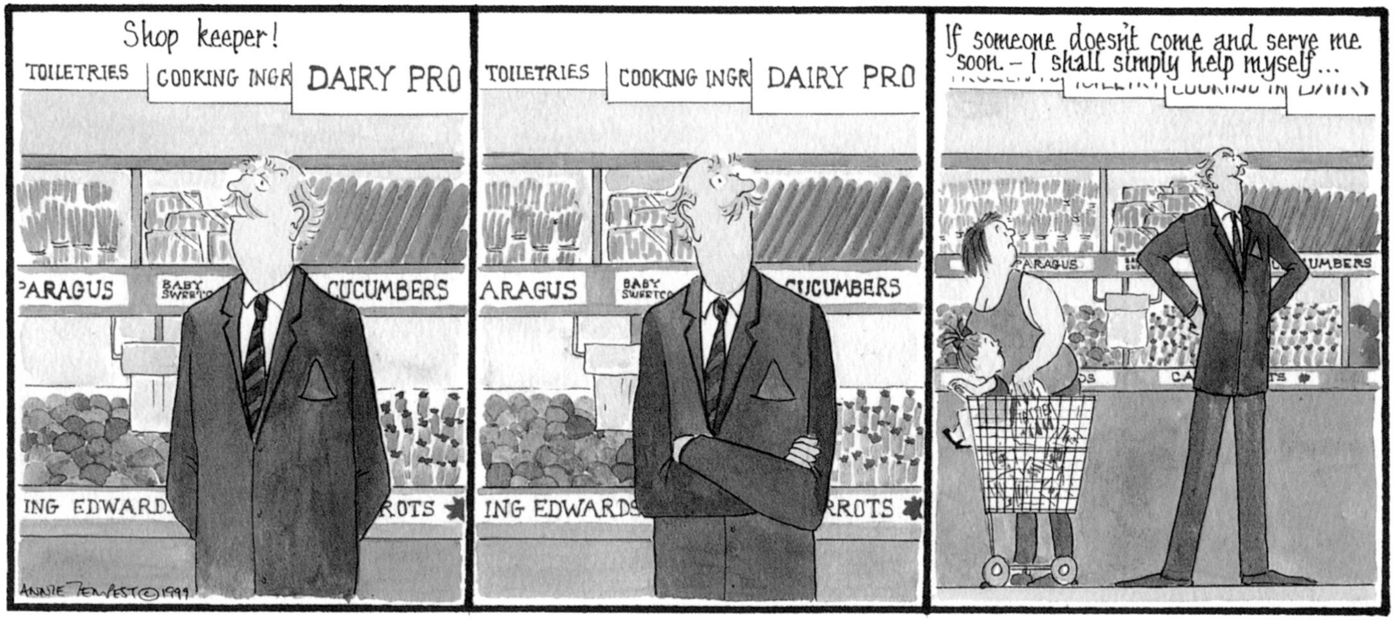
Shop keeper!
TOILETRIES
COOKING INGR
DAIRY PRO
ARAGUS
CUCUMBERS
ING EDWARDS
RROTS
ANNIE TEMPEST © 1999
TOILETRIES
COOKING INGR
DAIRY PRO
ARAGUS
CUCUMBERS
ING EDWARDS
RROTS
If someone doesn't come and serve me soon. – I shall simply help myself...

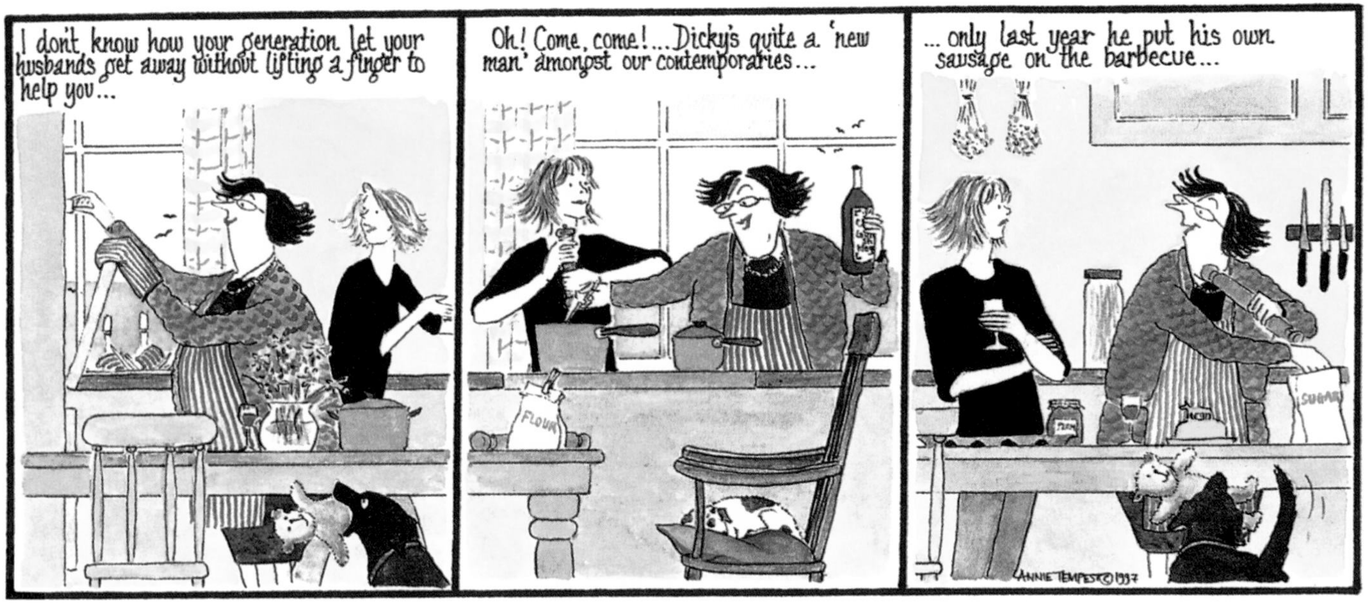
I don't know how your generation let your husbands get away without lifting a finger to help you...
Oh! Come, come!... Dicky's quite a 'new man' amongst our contemporaries...
...only last year he put his own sausage on the barbecue...
ANNIE TEMPEST © 1997

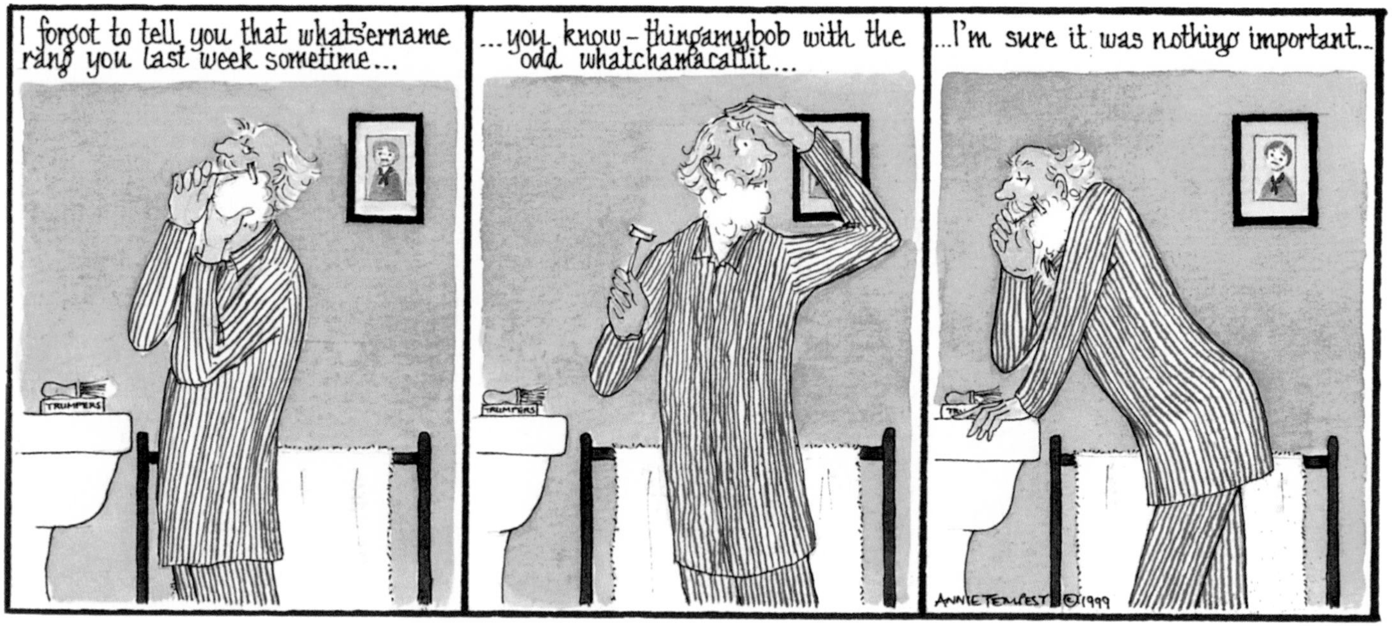
I forgot to tell you that whats'ername rang you last week sometime...
...you know – thingamybob with the odd whatchamacallit...
...I'm sure it was nothing important...
TRUMPERS
TRUMPERS
ANNIE TEMPEST ©1999

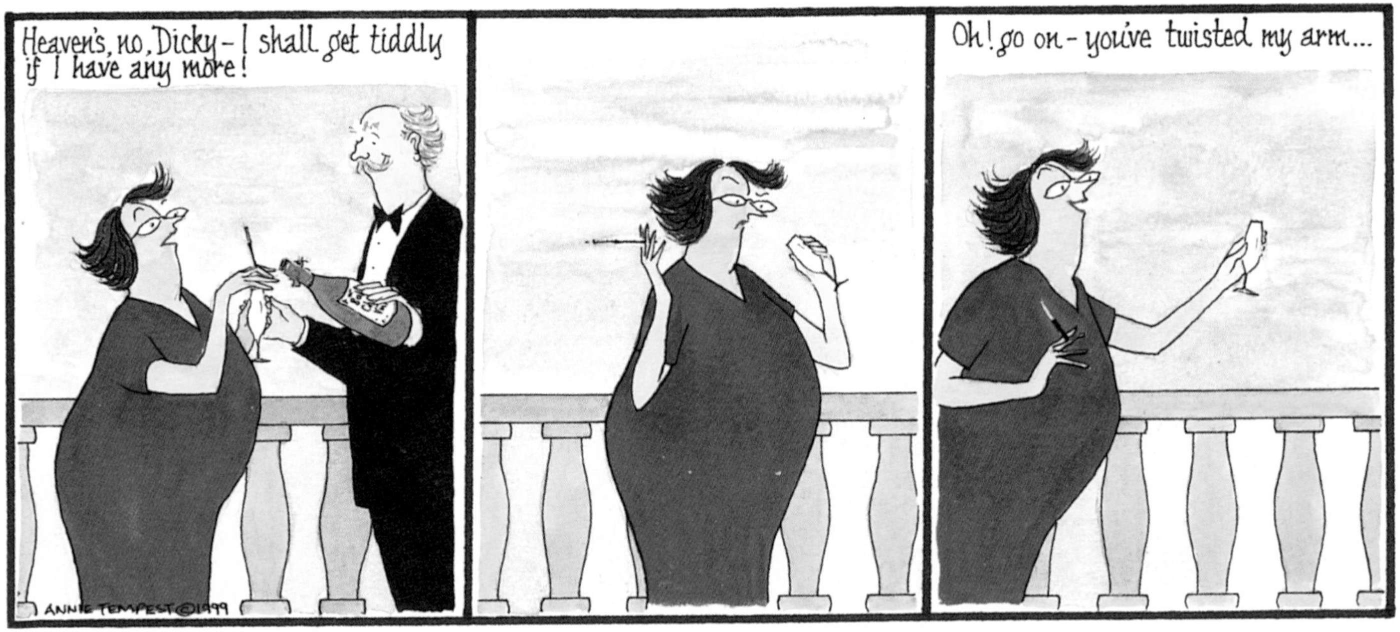
Heaven's, no, Dicky – I shall get tiddly if I have any more!
ANNIE TEMPEST ©1999
Oh! go on – you've twisted my arm...

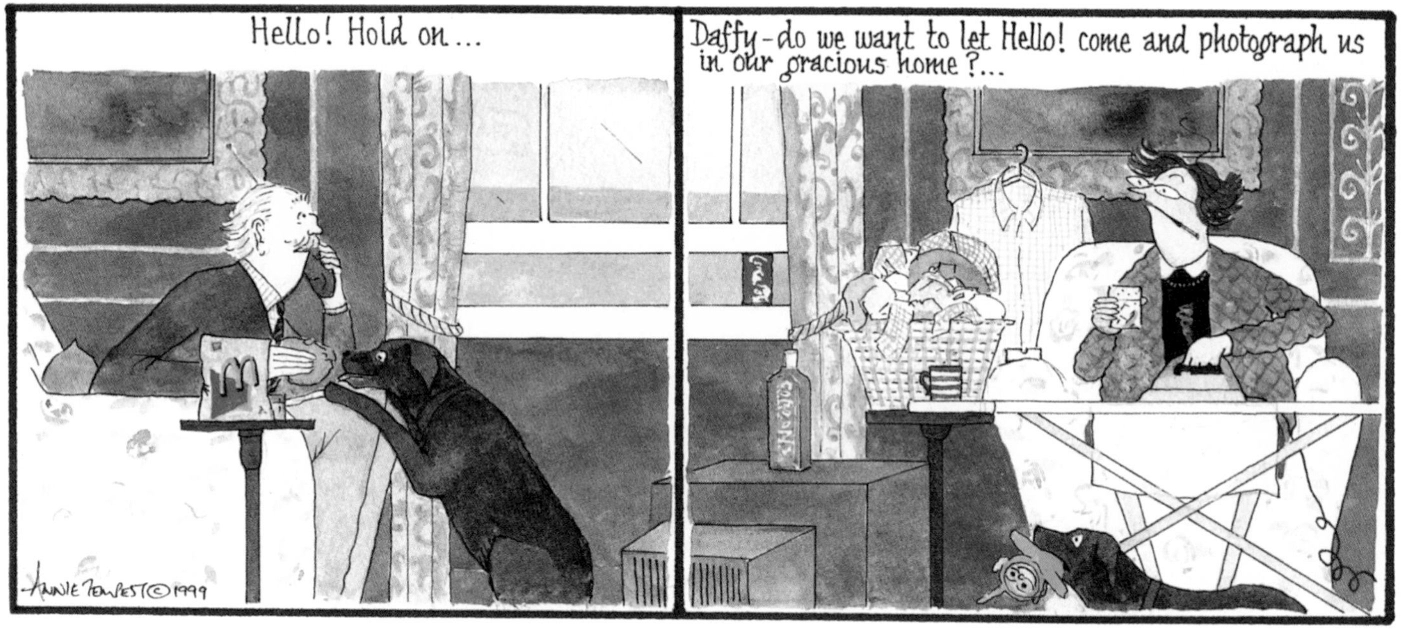
Hello! Hold on...
Daffy - do we want to let Hello! come and photograph us in our gracious home?...
ANNIE TEMPEST © 1999

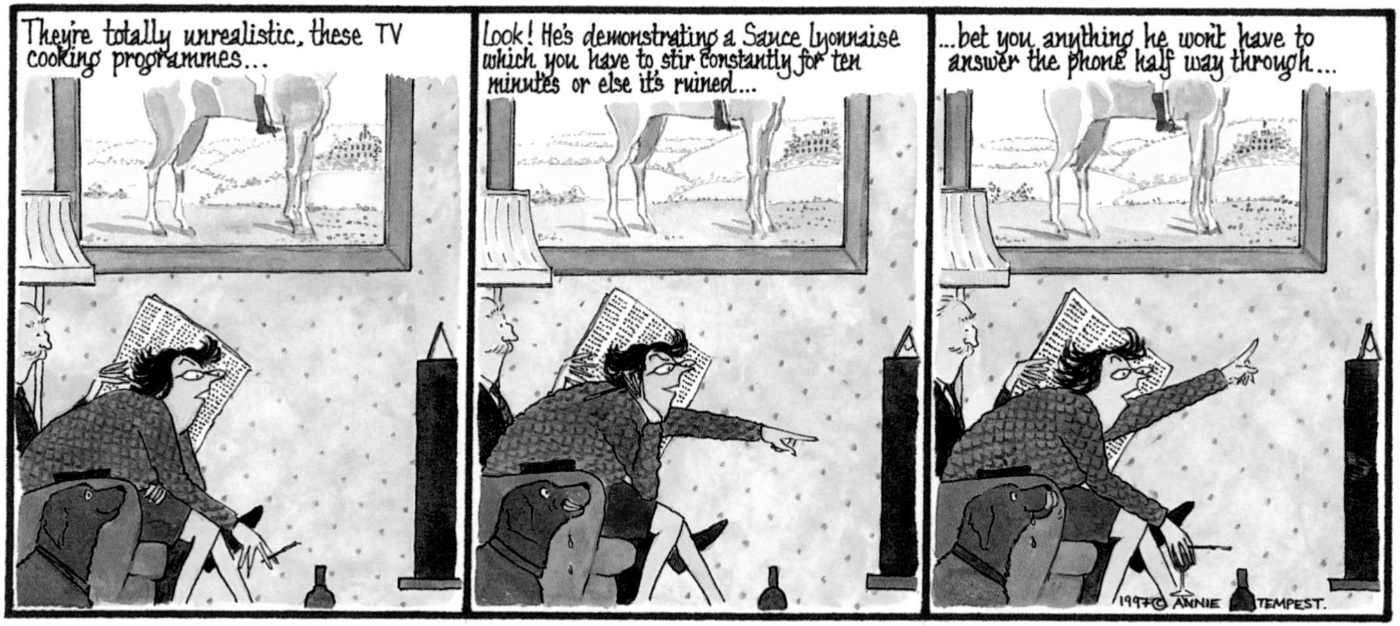
They're totally unrealistic, these TV cooking programmes...
Look! He's demonstrating a Sauce Lyonnaise which you have to stir constantly for ten minutes or else it's ruined...
...bet you anything he won't have to answer the phone half way through...
1997 © ANNIE TEMPEST.

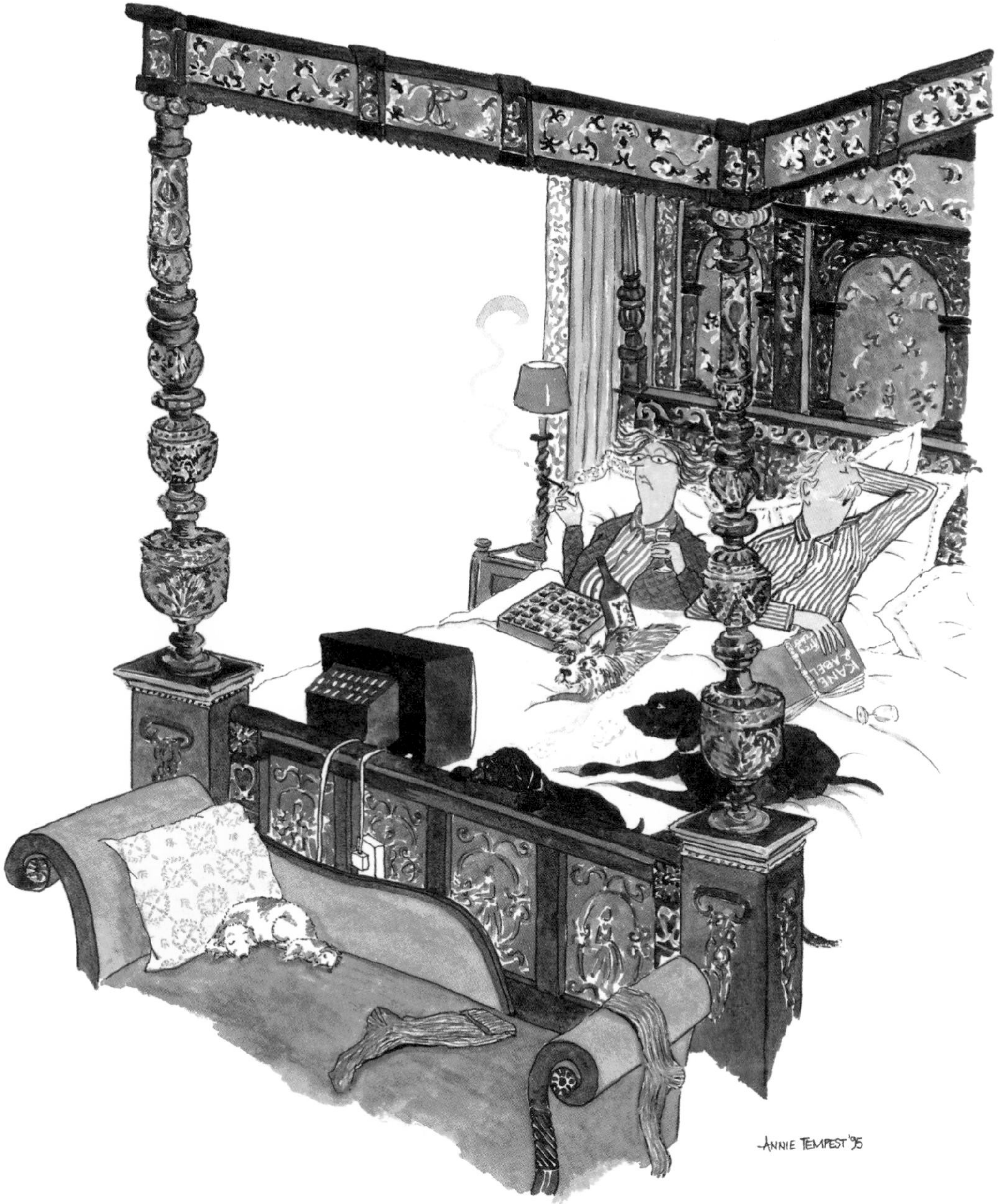
KANE & ABEL
ANNIE TEMPEST '95

"I don't think the bed scenes are very realistic..."

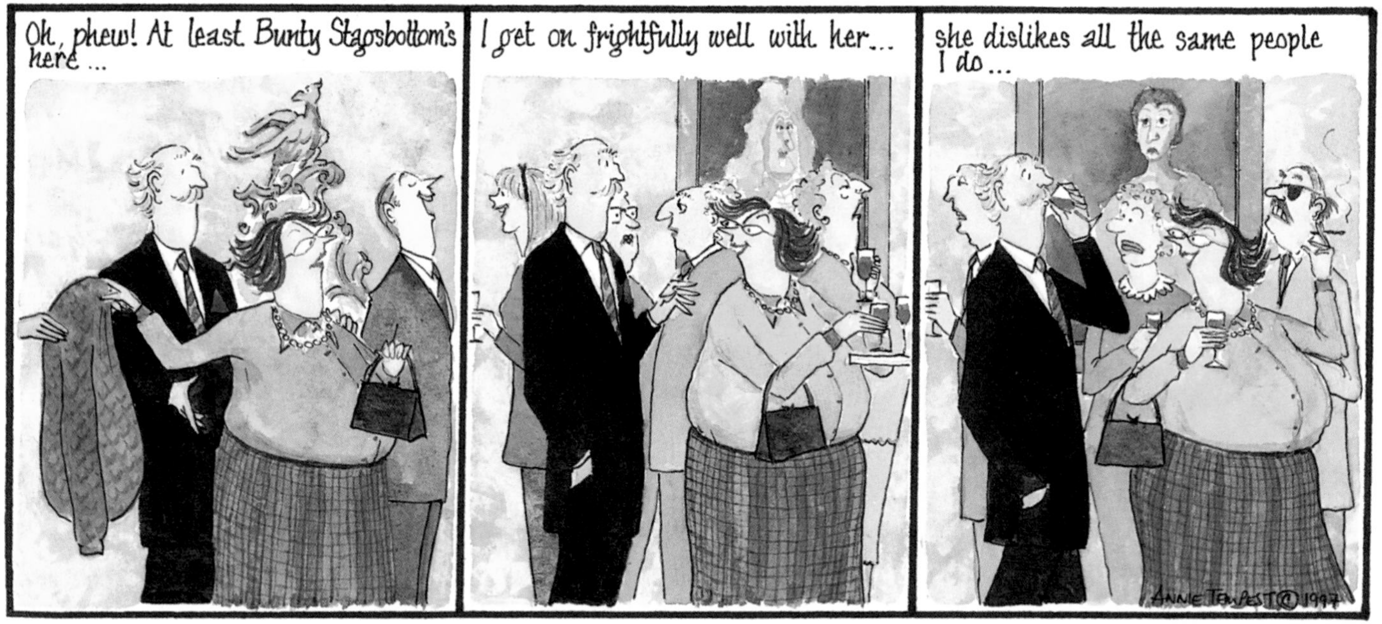
Oh, phew! At least Bunty Stagsbottom's here ...
I get on frightfully well with her...
she dislikes all the same people I do...
ANNIE TEMPEST © 1997

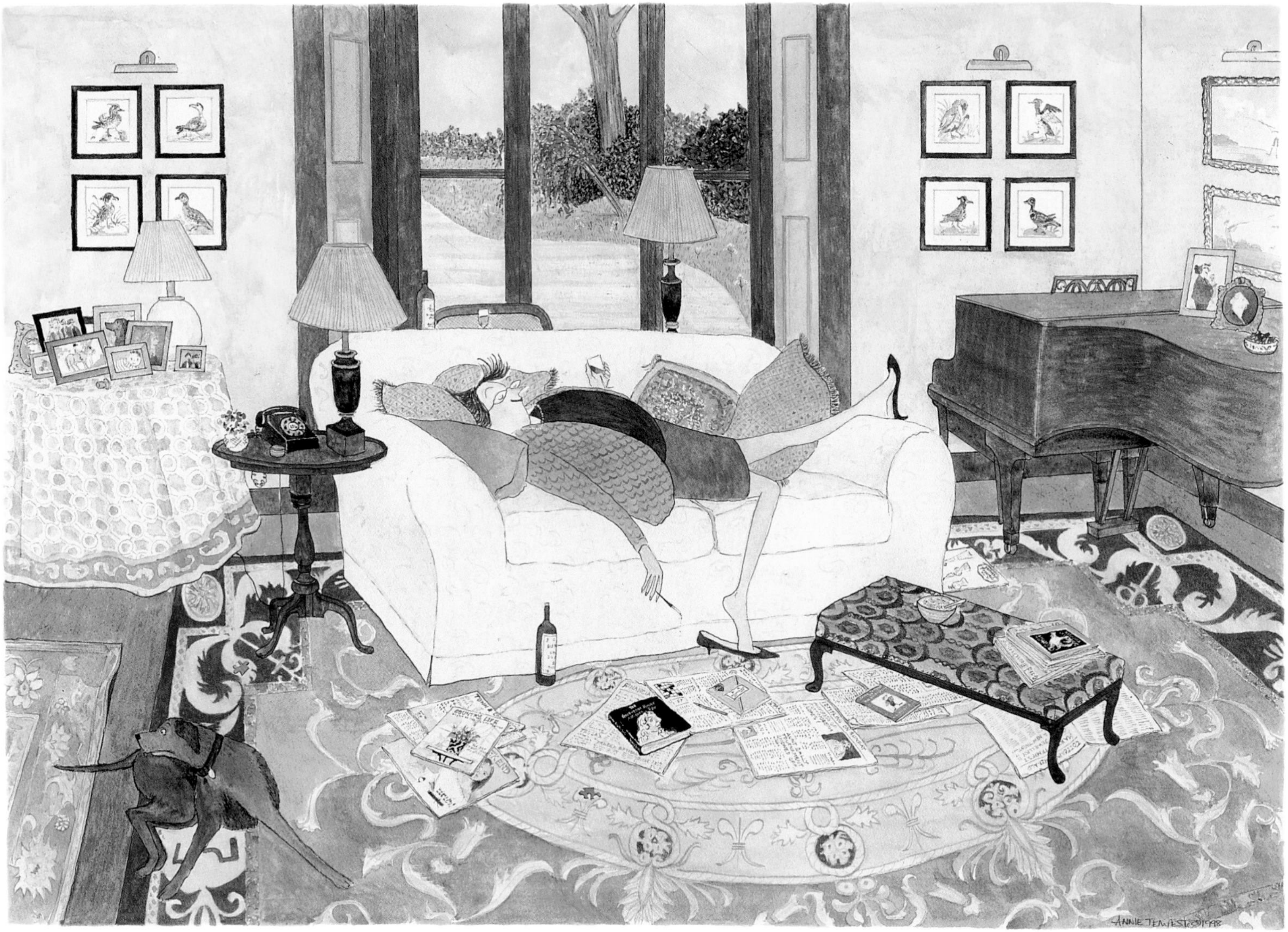

THE FEMALE CHARACTER – A tendancy to steal 5 minutes rest after the children have grown up...

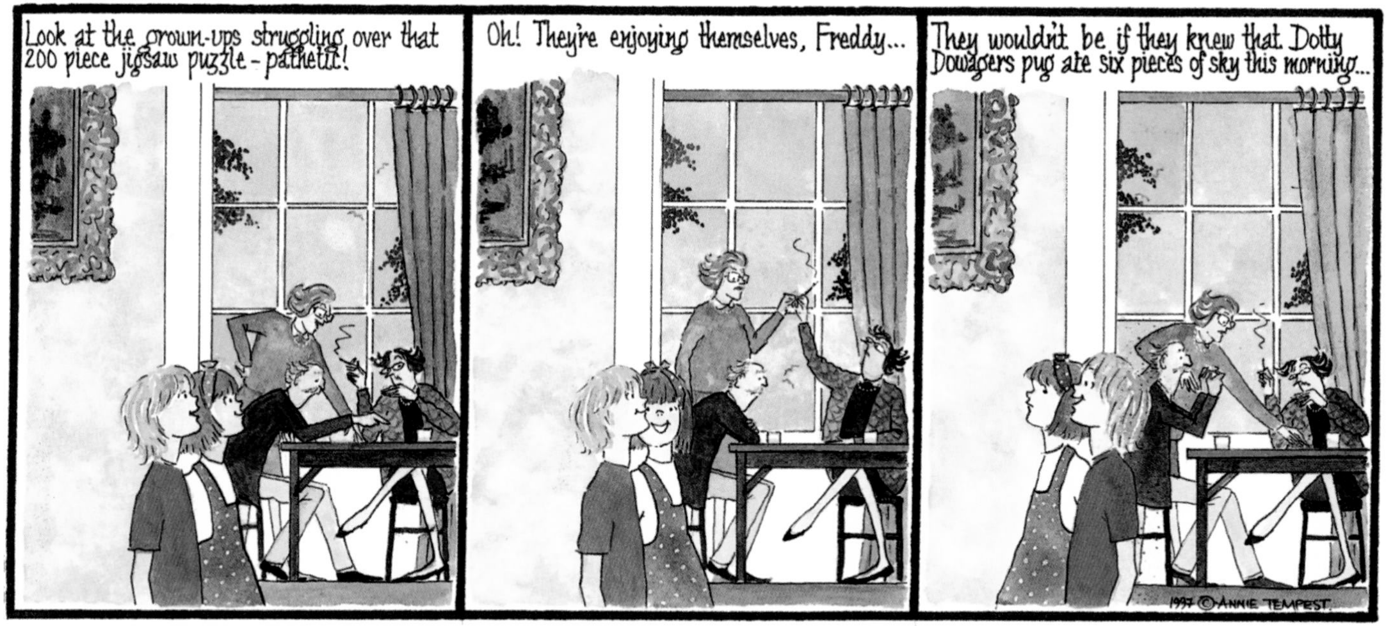
Look at the grown-ups struggling over that 200 piece jigsaw puzzle - pathetic!
Oh! They're enjoying themselves, Freddy...
They wouldn't be if they knew that Dotty Dowagers pug ate six pieces of sky this morning...
1997 © ANNIE TEMPEST

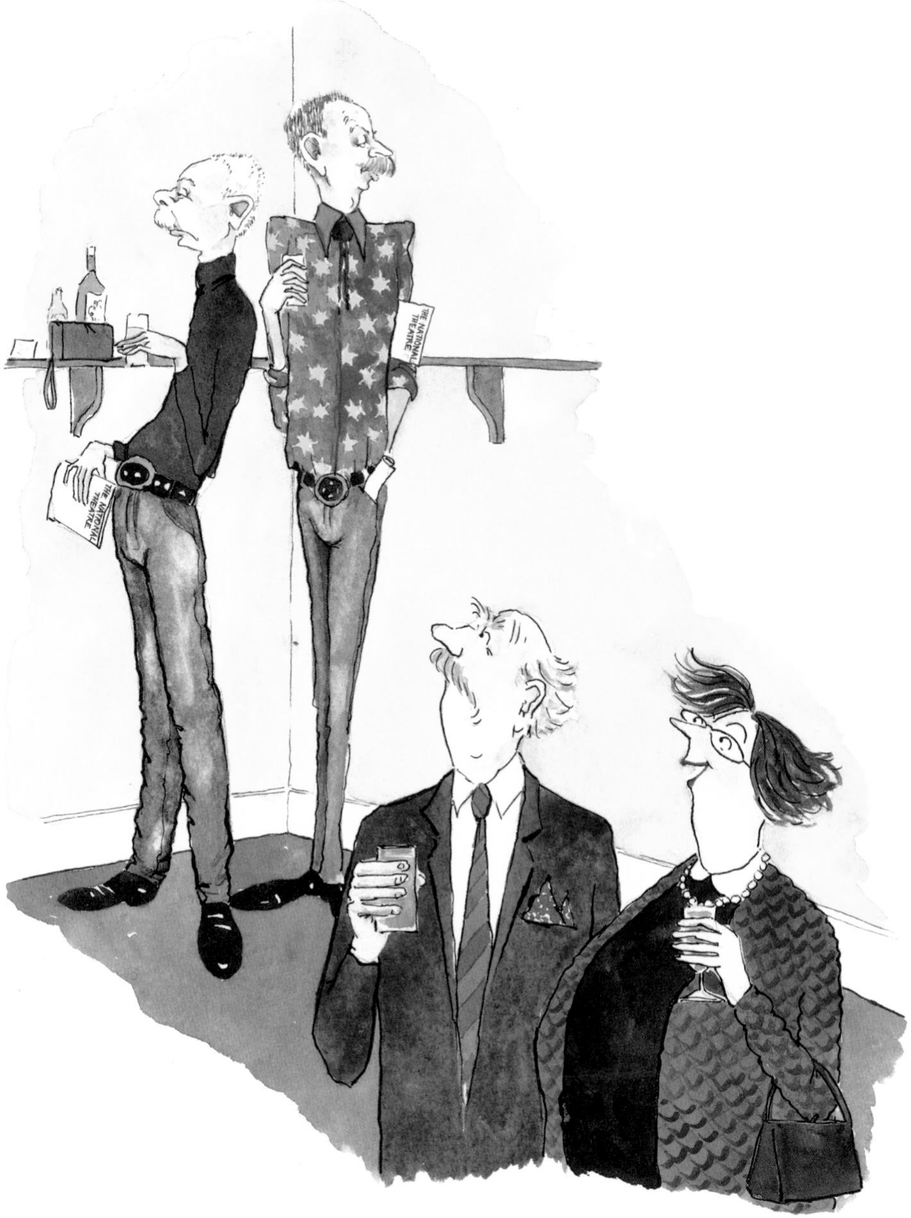
THE NATIONAL THEATRE
THE NATIONAL THEATRE

"How fascinating-do you think they have coming out dances, Dicky?.."

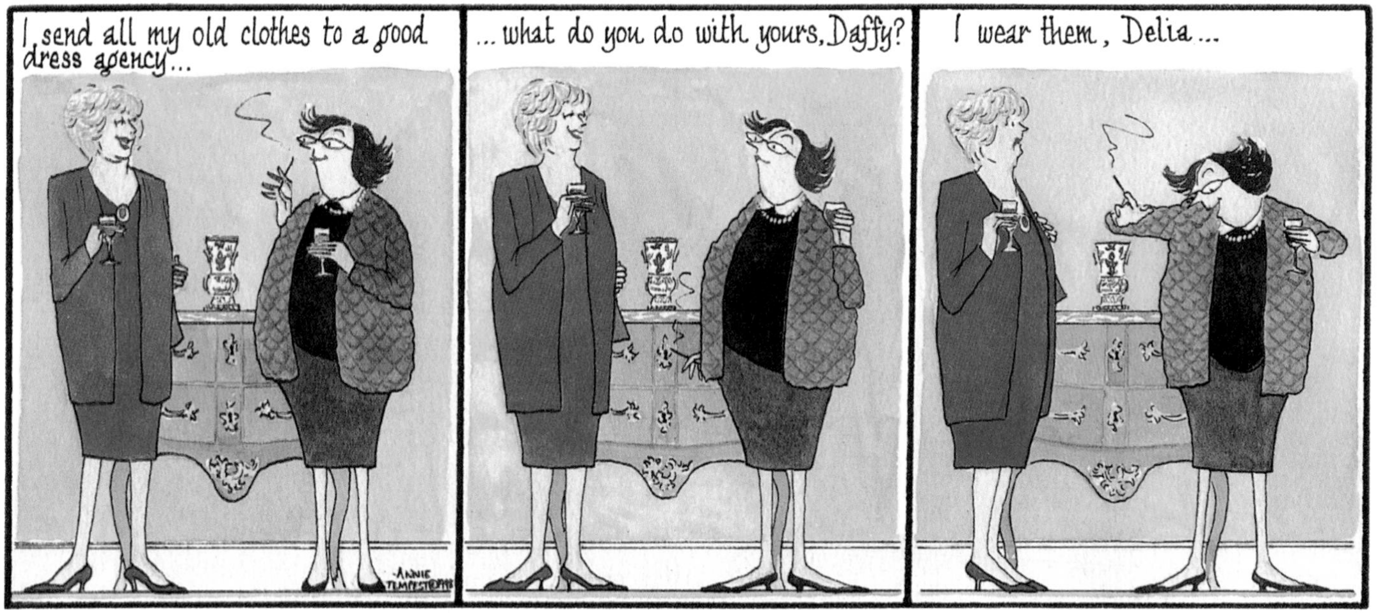
I send all my old clothes to a good dress agency...
... what do you do with yours, Daffy?
I wear them, Delia...
ANNIE TEMPEST

THE FEMALE CHARACTER — The ability to see facts from whichever angle suits them best.

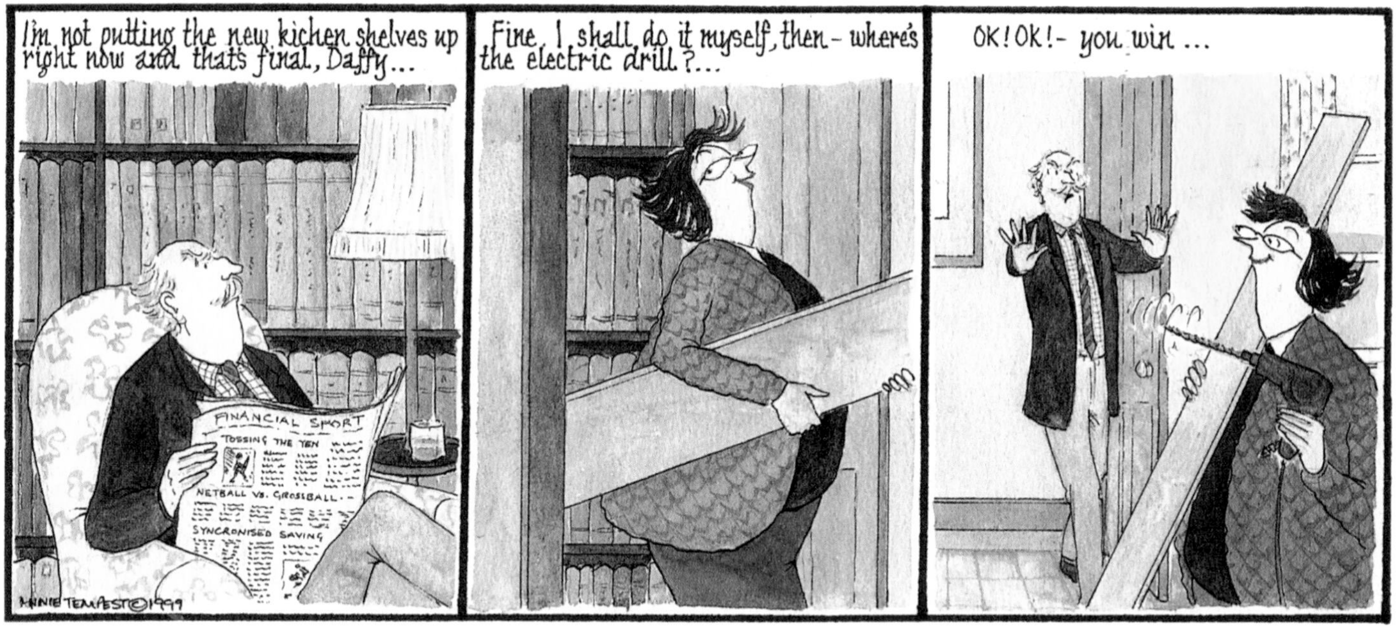
I'm not putting the new kichen shelves up right now and that's final, Daffy...
FINANCIAL SPORT
TOSSING THE TEN
NETBALL VS. CROSSBALL -
SYNCRONISED SAVING
ANNIE TEMPEST © 1999
Fine, I shall do it myself, then - where's the electric drill?...
OK! OK! - you win ...

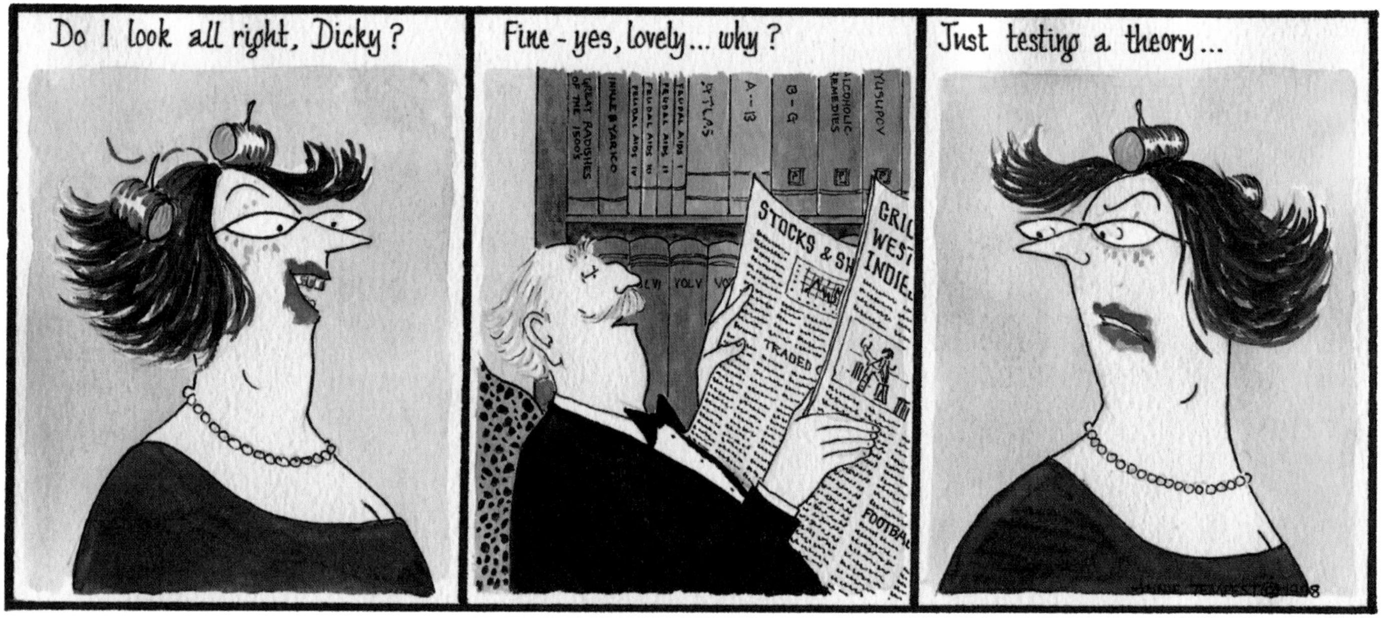
Do I look all right, Dicky?
Fine - yes, lovely... why?
Just testing a theory...

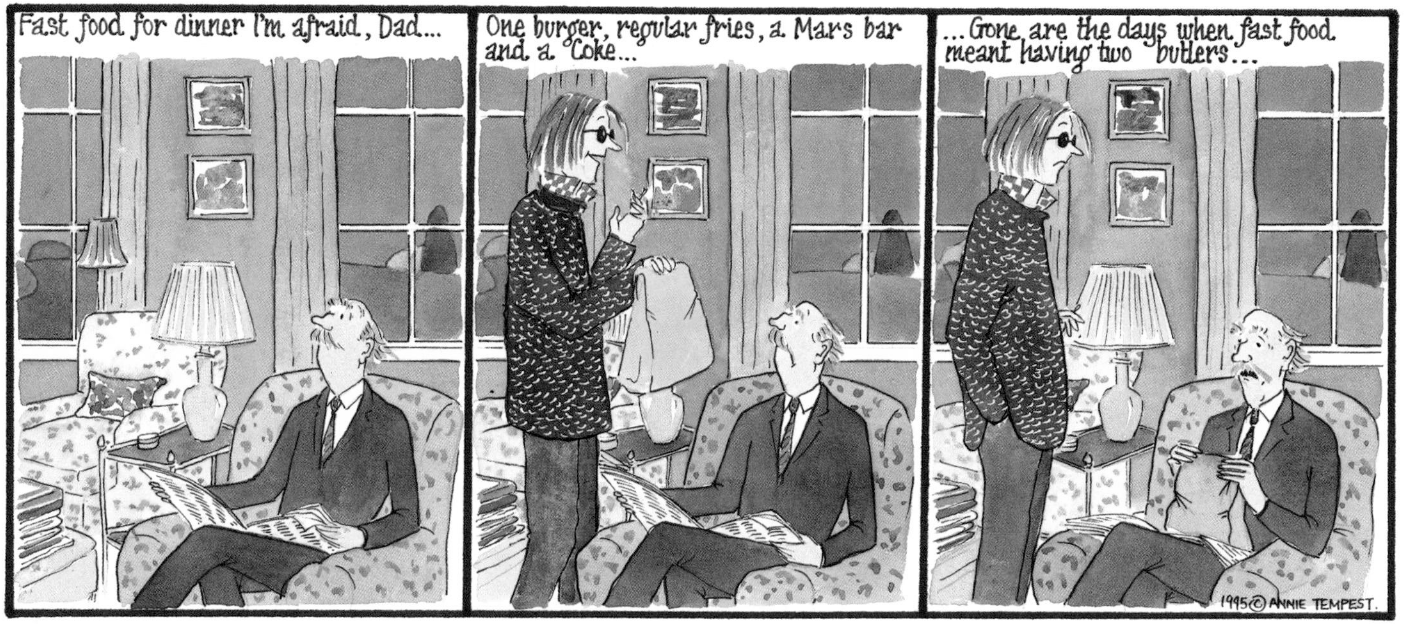
Fast food for dinner I'm afraid, Dad....
One burger, regular fries, a Mars bar and a Coke...
...Gone are the days when fast food meant having two butlers...
1995 © ANNIE TEMPEST.

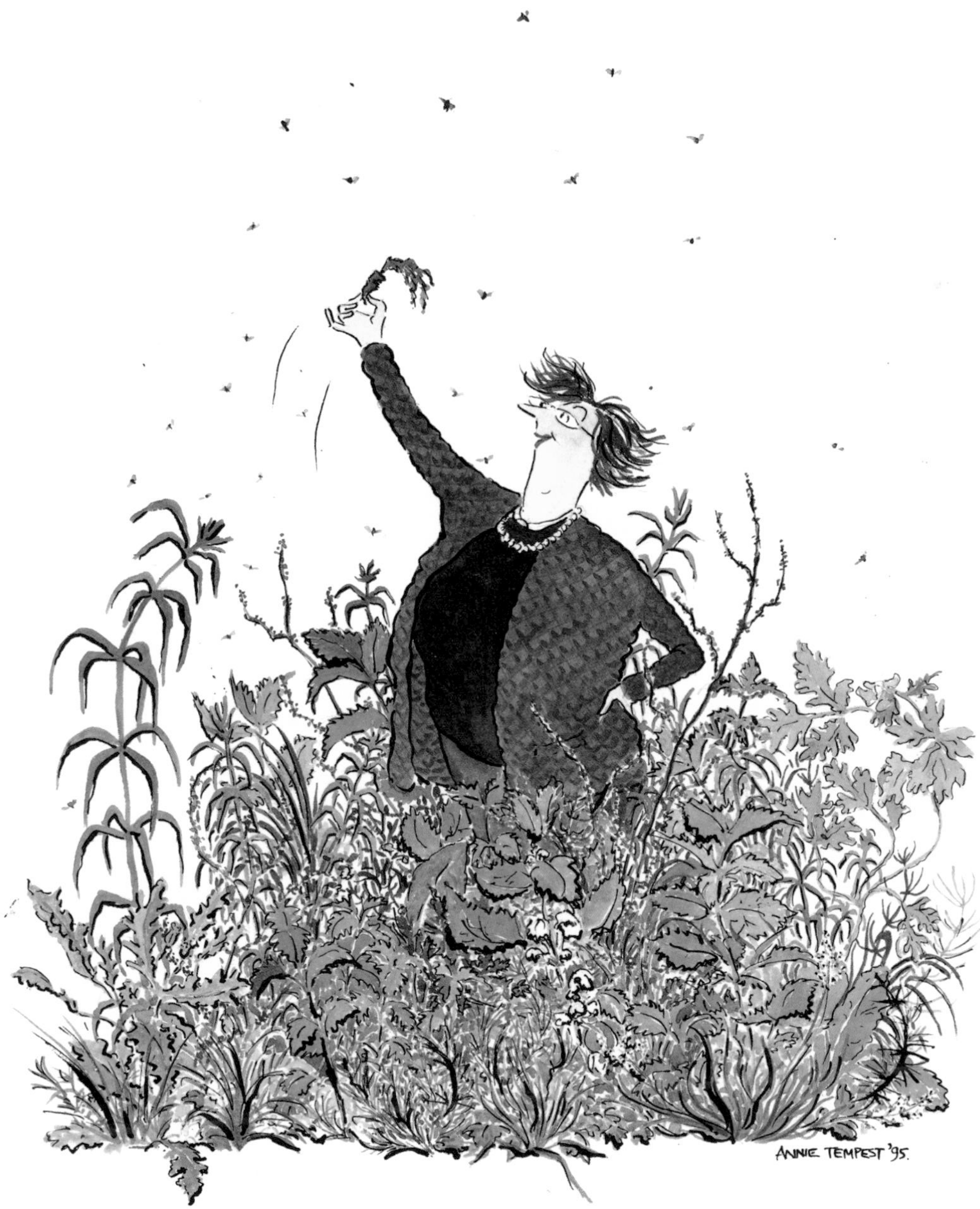
ANNIE TEMPEST '95.

" OUR FIRST ORGANIC CARROT, DICKY!..."

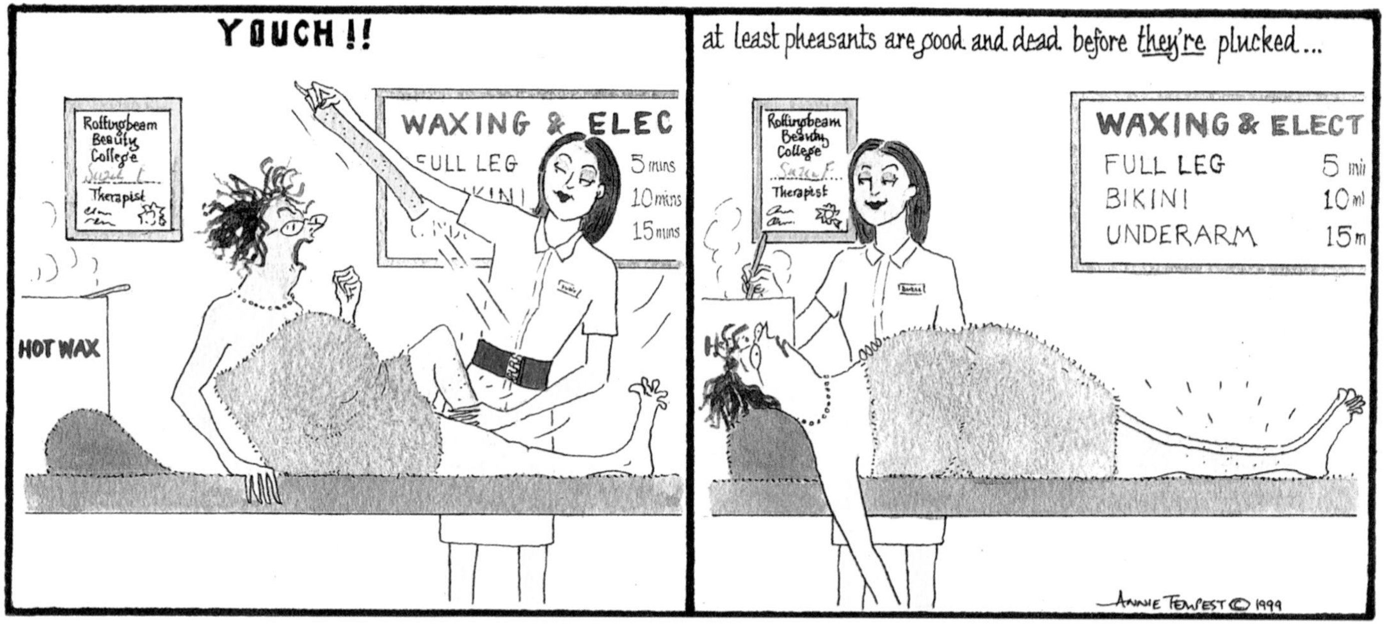
YOUCH!!
Rollingbeam Beauty College
Therapist
WAXING & ELEC
FULL LEG 5 mins
10 mins
15 mins
HOT WAX
at least pheasants are good and dead before they're plucked...
Rollingbeam Beauty College
Therapist
WAXING & ELECT
FULL LEG 5
BIKINI 10
UNDERARM 15
ANNIE TEMPEST © 1999

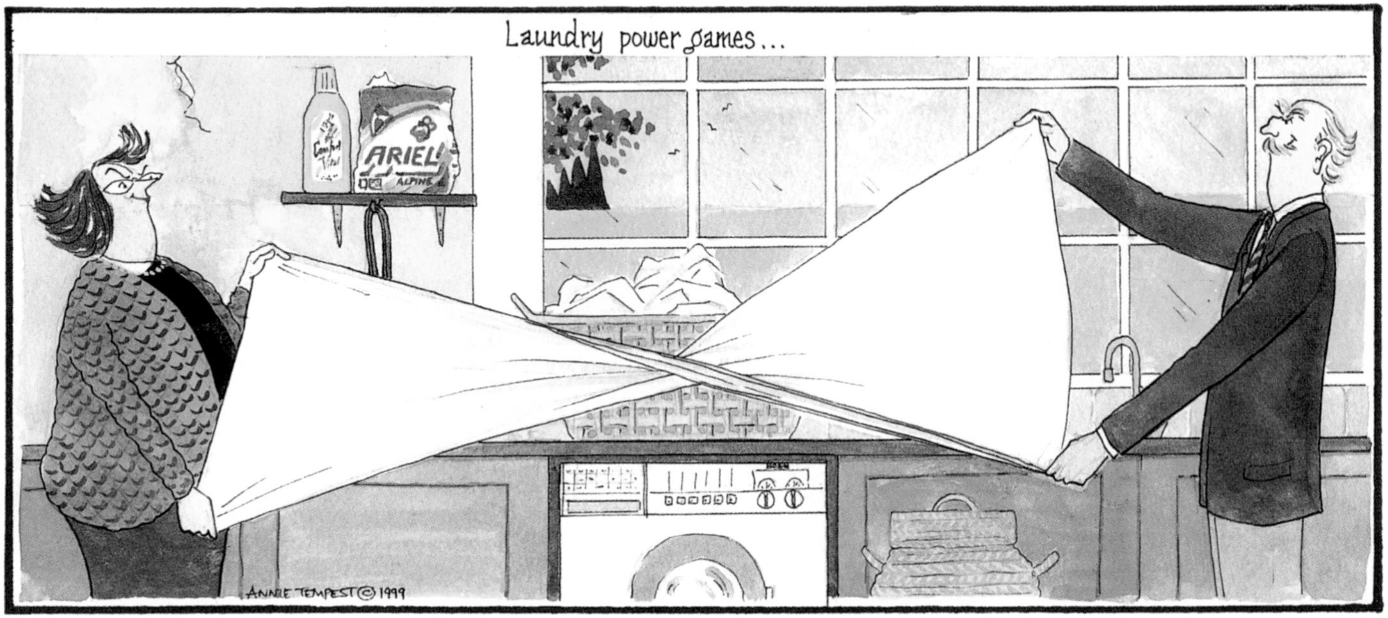
ARIEL
ALPINE
ANNIE TEMPEST © 1999

Laundry power games...

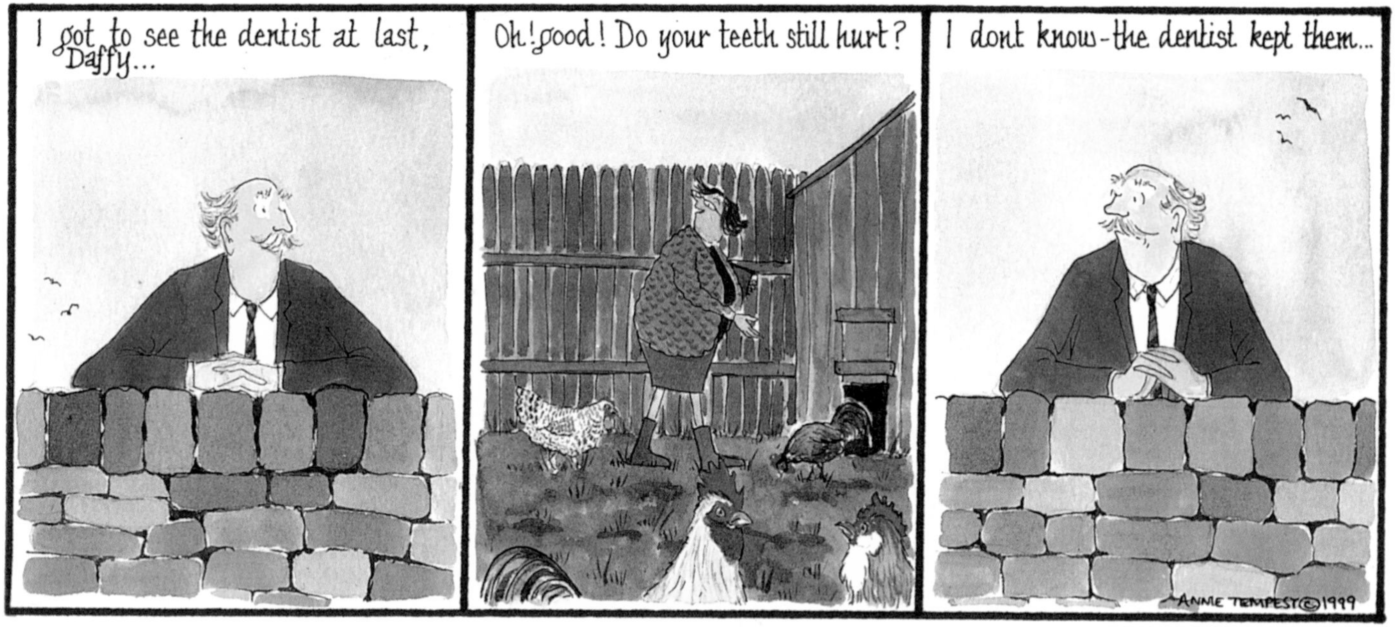
I got to see the dentist at last, Daffy...
Oh! good! Do your teeth still hurt?
I dont know - the dentist kept them...
ANNE TEMPEST © 1999

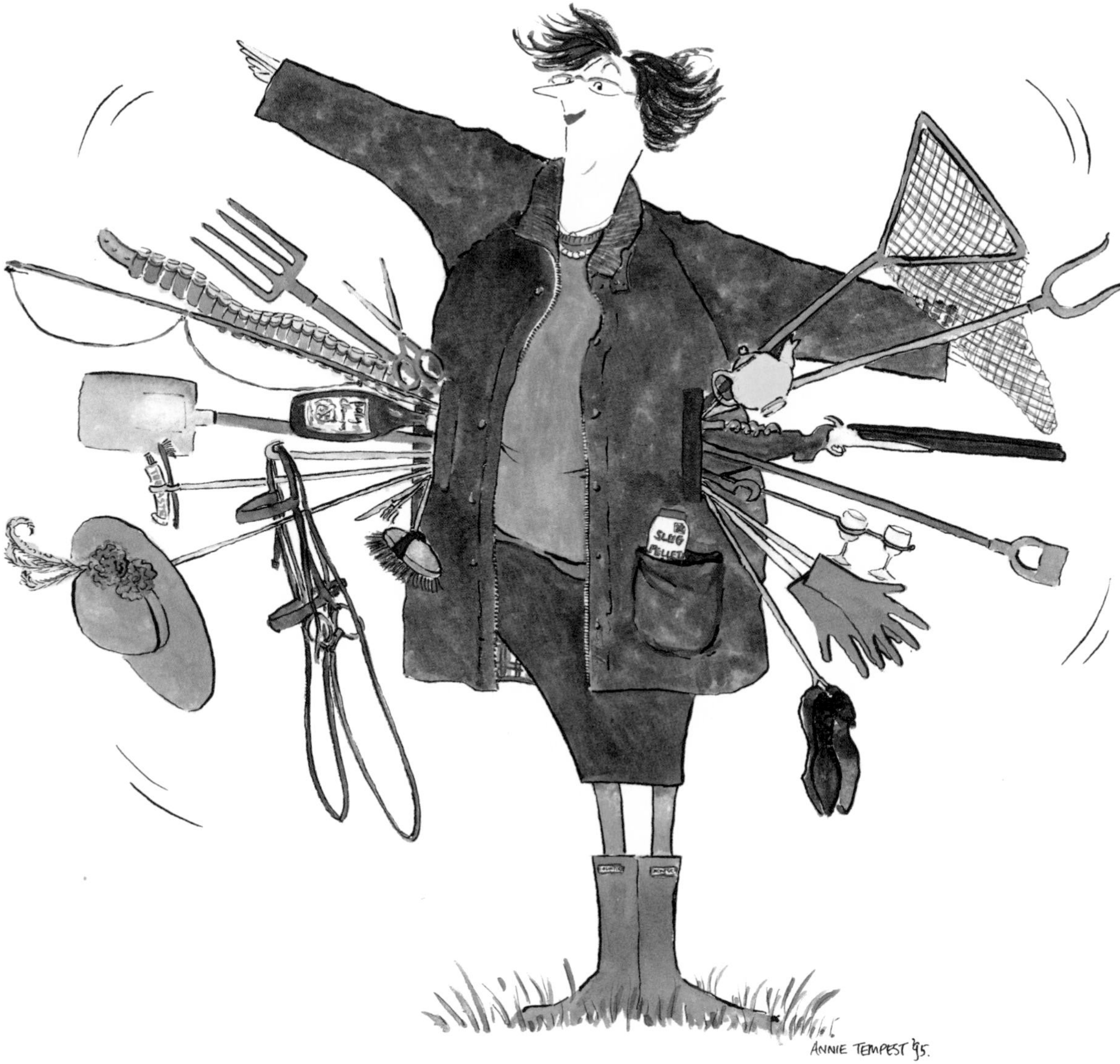
ANNIE TEMPEST '95.

SWISS ARMY BARBOUR...

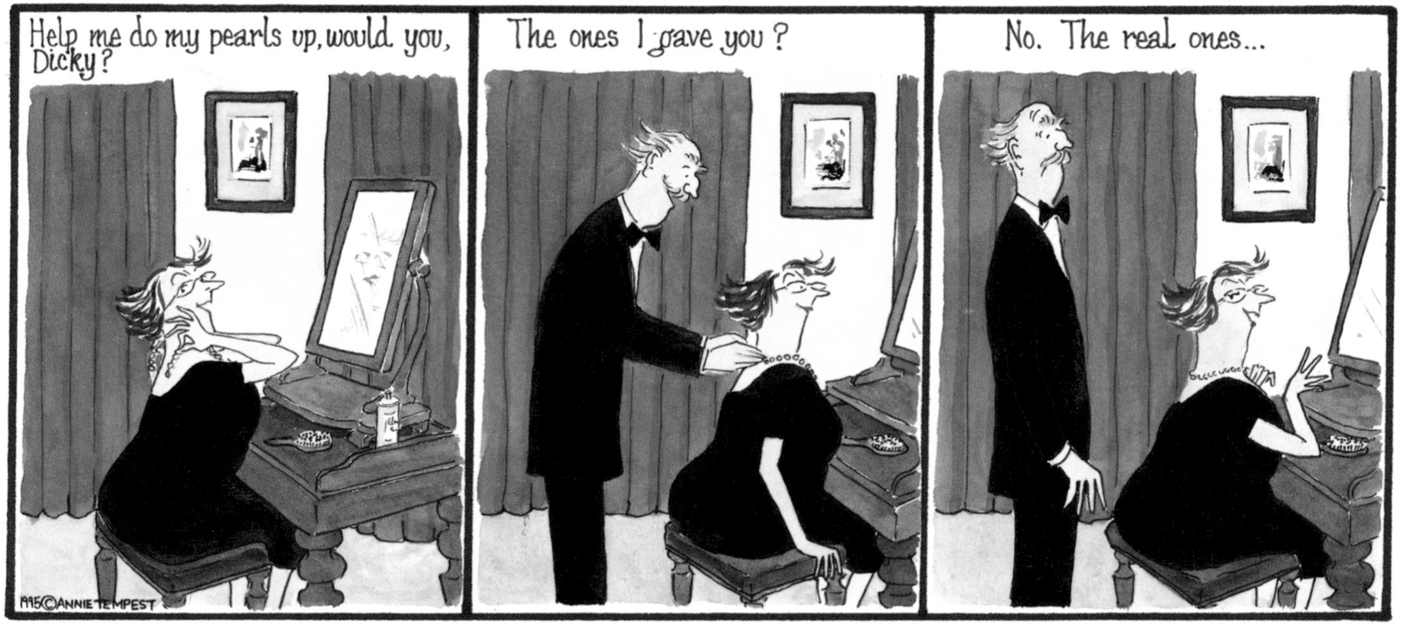
Help me do my pearls up, would you, Dicky?
The ones I gave you?
No. The real ones...
1995 © ANNIE TEMPEST

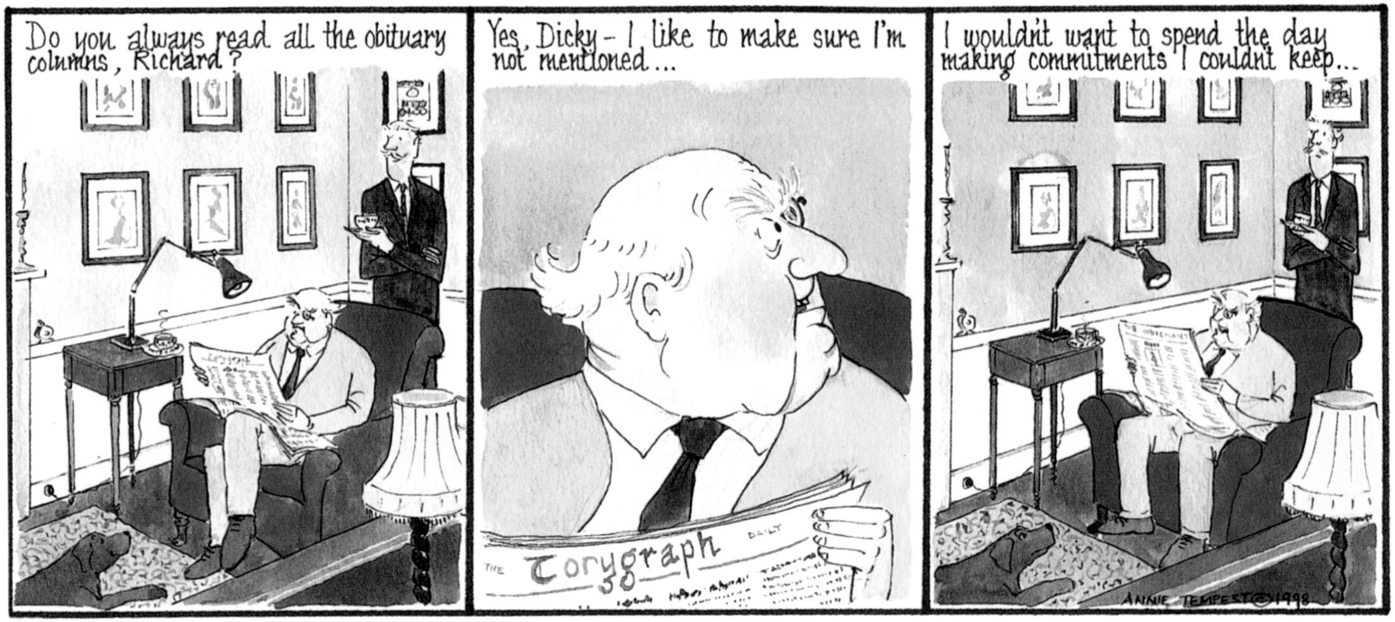
Do you always read all the obituary columns, Richard?
Yes, Dicky – I like to make sure I'm not mentioned...
The Torygraph
I wouldn't want to spend the day making commitments I couldn't keep...
ANNIE TEMPEST © 1998

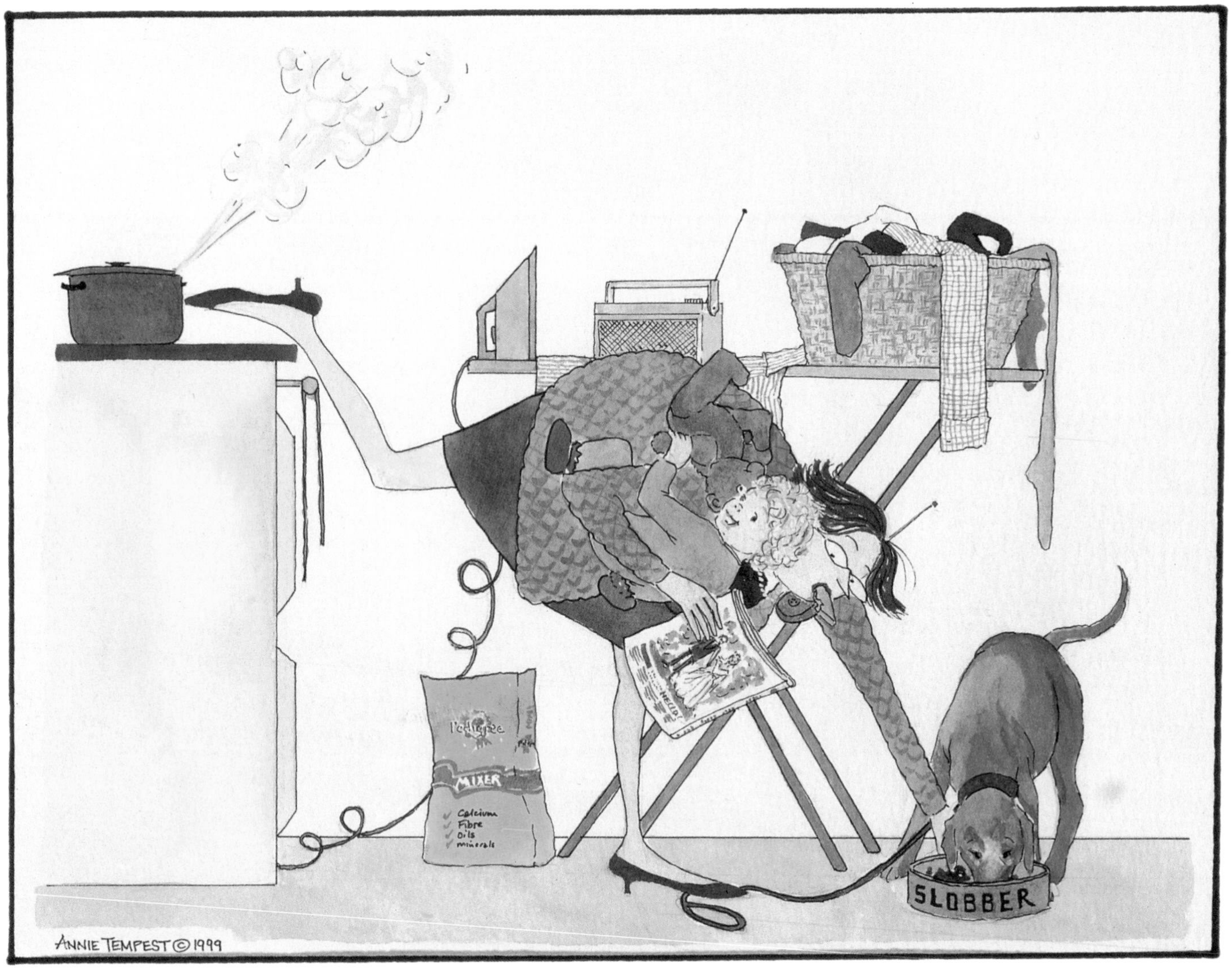
Pedigree
MIXER
Calcium
Fibre
Oils
minerals
SLOBBER
ANNIE TEMPEST © 1999

THE FEMALE CHARACTER: A predilection for doing six things at once...

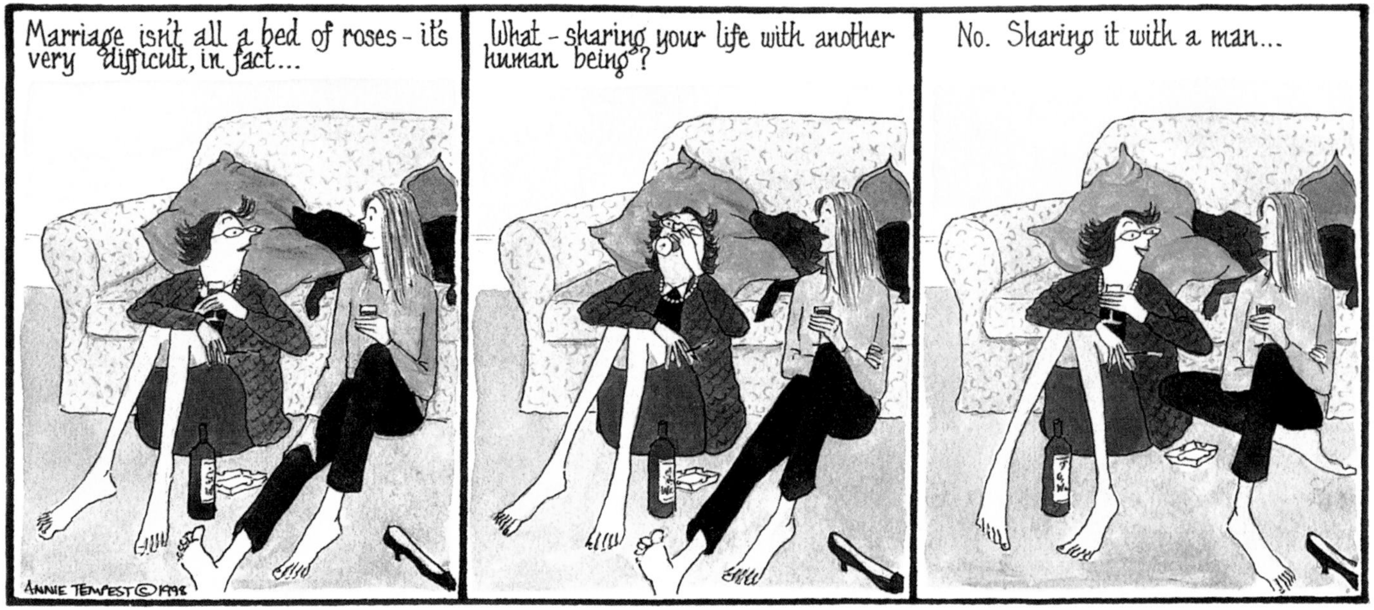
Marriage isn't all a bed of roses - it's very difficult, in fact...
ANNIE TEMPEST © 1998
What - sharing your life with another human being?
No. Sharing it with a man...

Do you know that trick about putting a metal tea-spoon in a champagne bottle? It keeps the fizz in so you can save it until the next day...
No. What an extraordinary notion...
... we've never had an unfinished bottle...
ANNIE TEMPEST © 1998

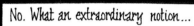

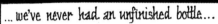

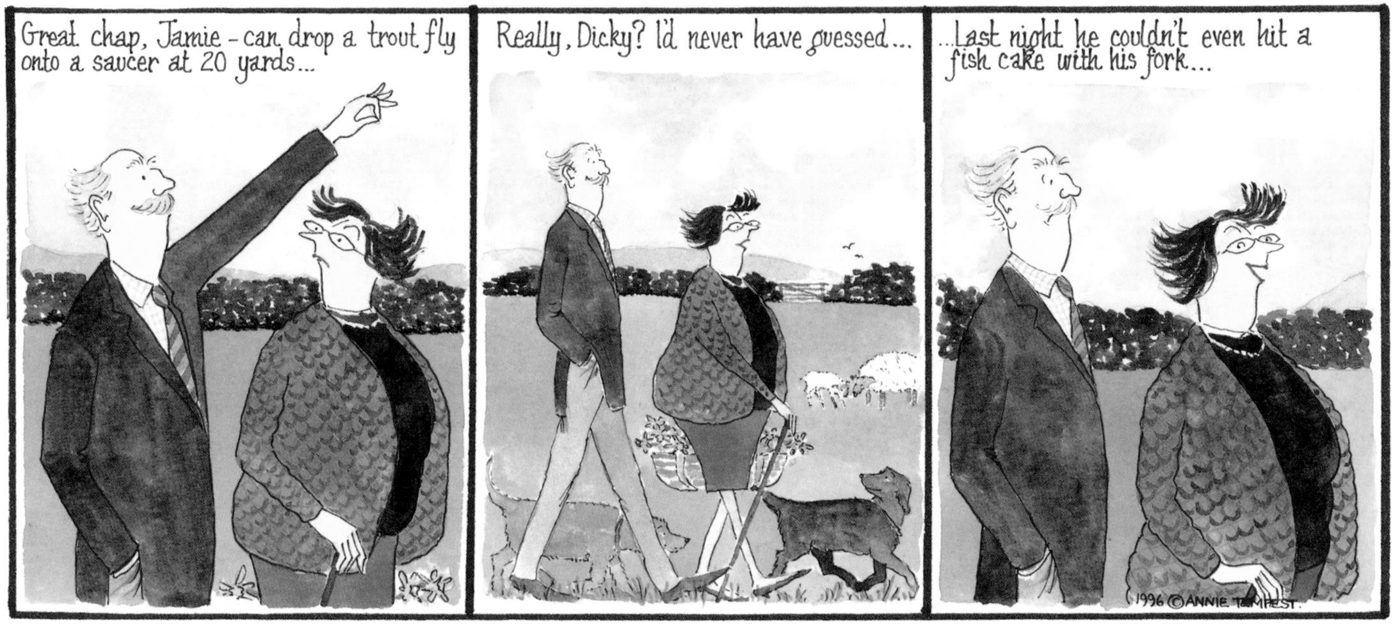
Great chap, Jamie - can drop a trout fly onto a saucer at 20 yards...
Really, Dicky? I'd never have guessed...
...Last night he couldn't even hit a fish cake with his fork...
1996 © ANNIE TEMPEST.

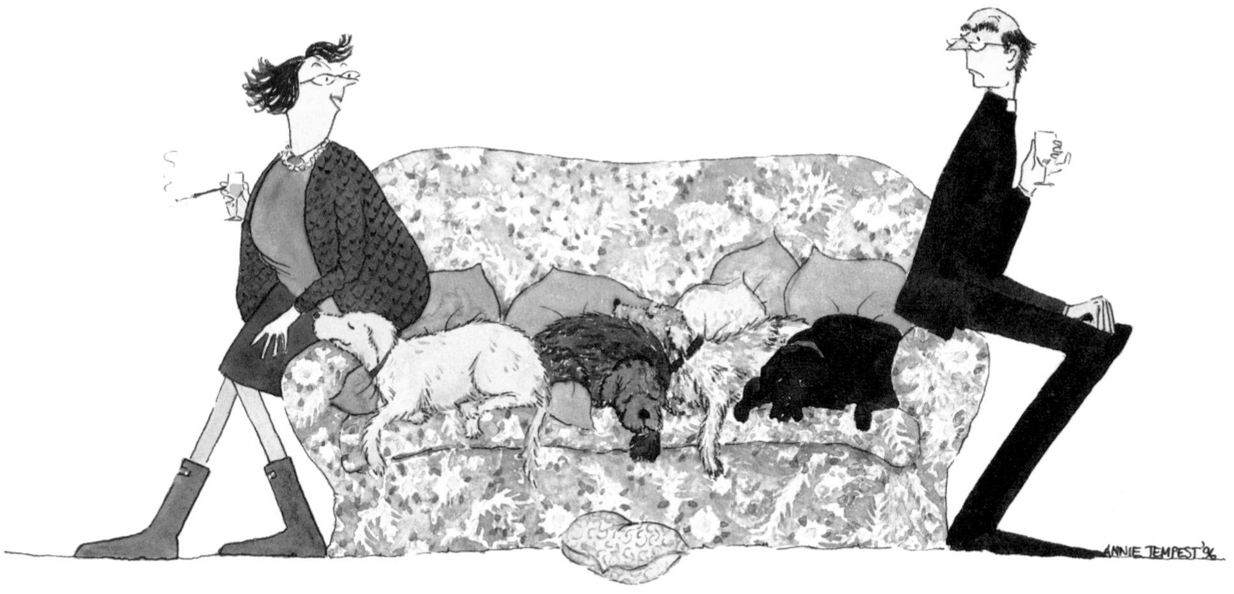
ANNIE TEMPEST '96

"More sherry, Vicar?"

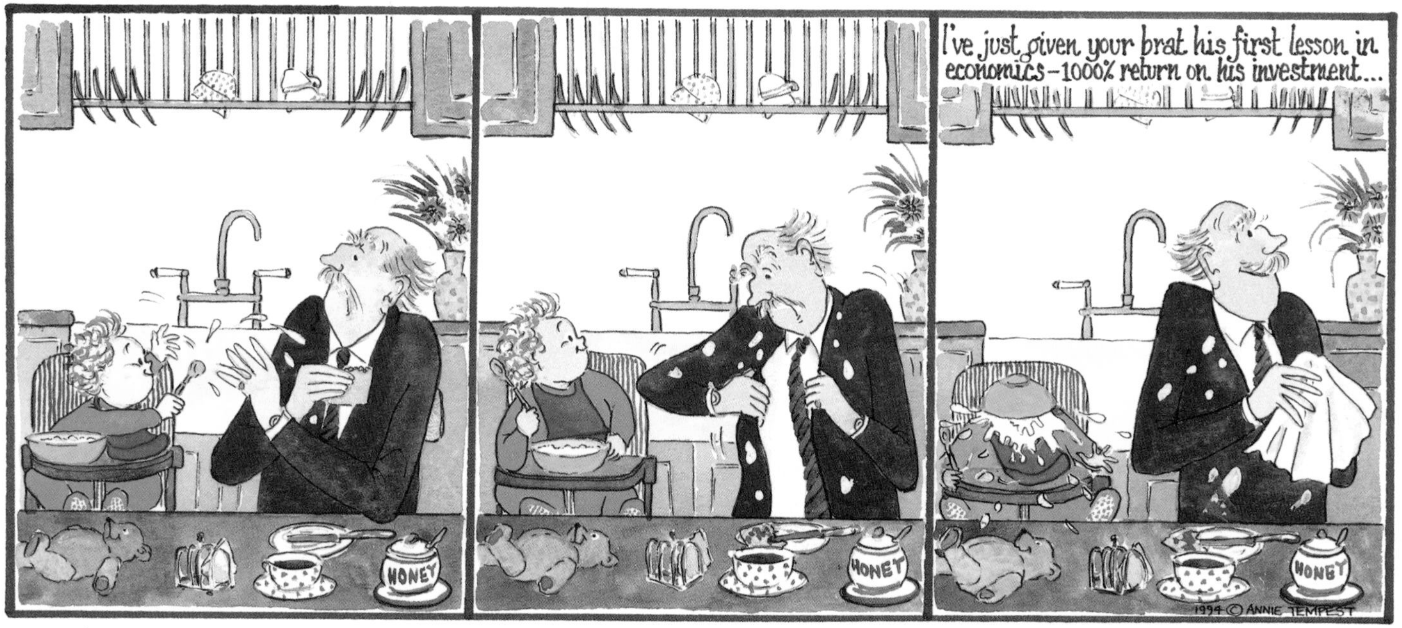
HONEY
HONEY
HONEY
I've just given your brat his first lesson in economics – 1000% return on his investment...
1994 © ANNIE TEMPEST

No-I can't invite the Harbinger-Harangues from Rattling-by-Furiously- it's too risky...

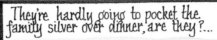

They're hardly going to pocket the family silver over dinner, are they?...

No. But they might well invite us back...

ANNIE TEMPEST © 2000

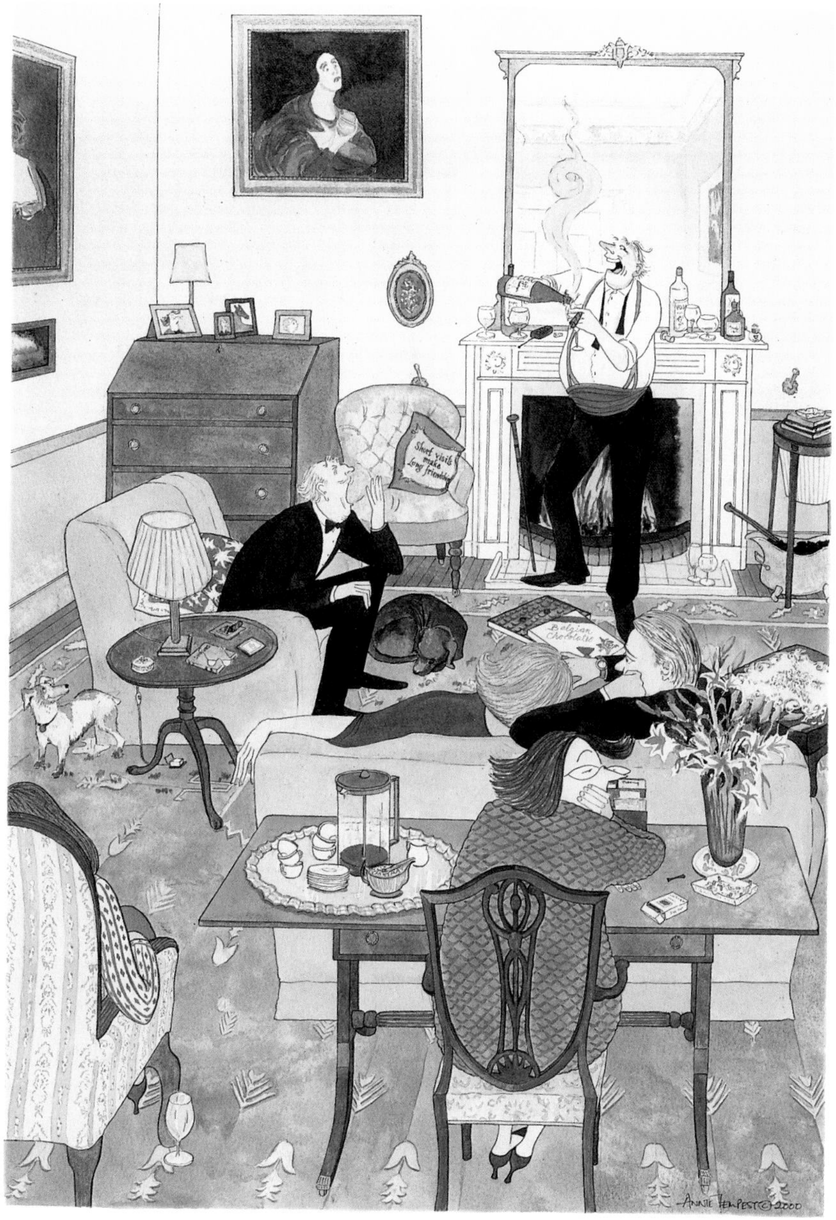
Short visits
make
Long
Belgian Chocolates
Annie Tempest © 2000

THE GUEST FROM HELL

The important business of warming the armchairs before the shooting party's return...

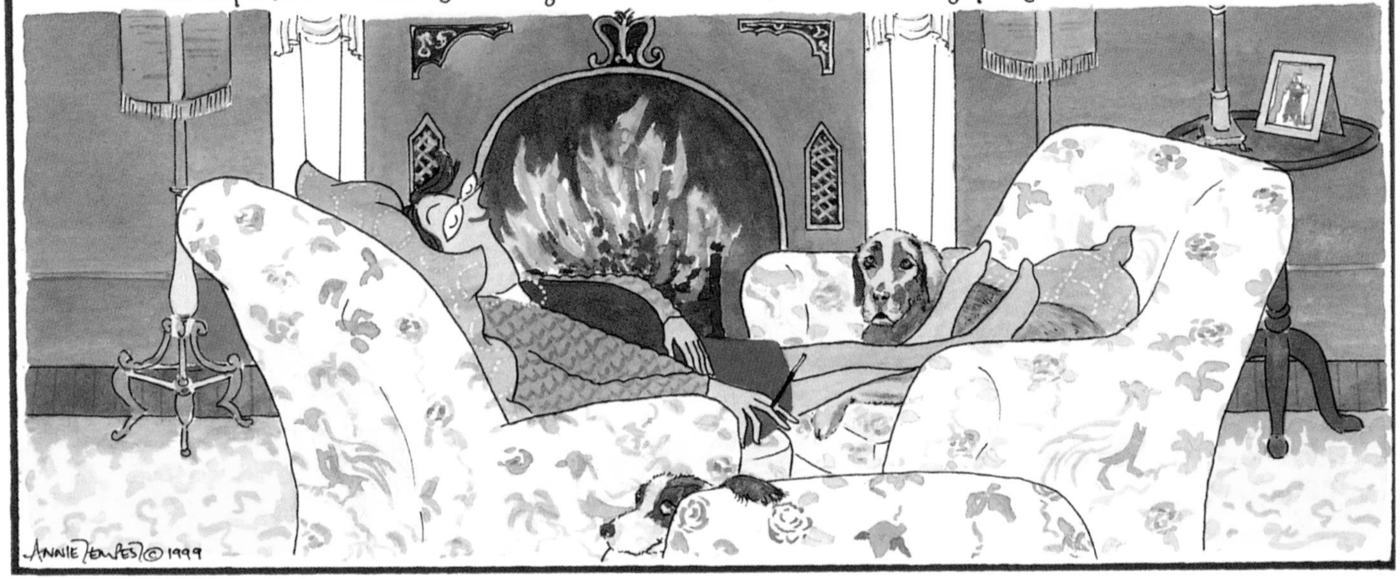
ANNIE TEMPEST © 1999

THE THREE AGES OF WOMAN

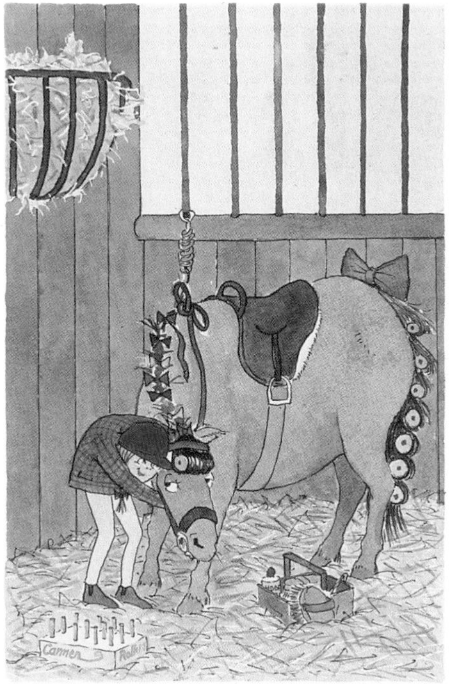
Carmen
Rollers

HORSES

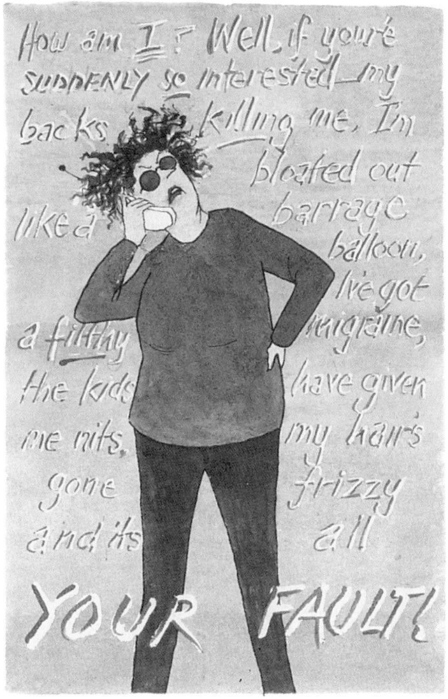
How am I? Well, if you're
SUDDENLY so interested, my
back's killing me. I'm
bloated out
like a barrage
balloon,
I've got
a filthy migraine,
the kids have given
me nits, my hair's
gone frizzy
and it's all
YOUR FAULT!

HORMONES

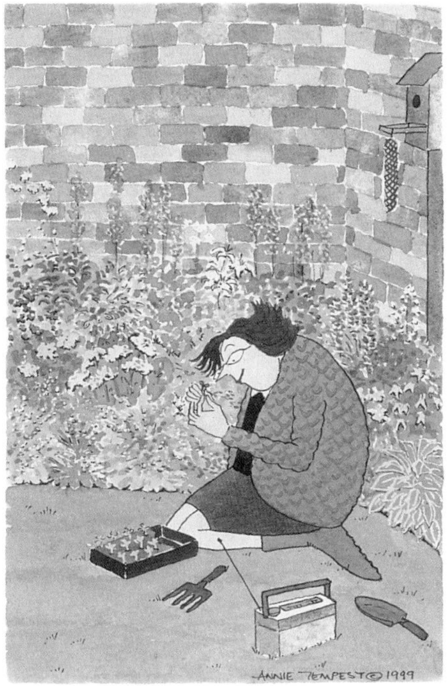
ANNIE TEMPEST © 1999

HORTICULTURE

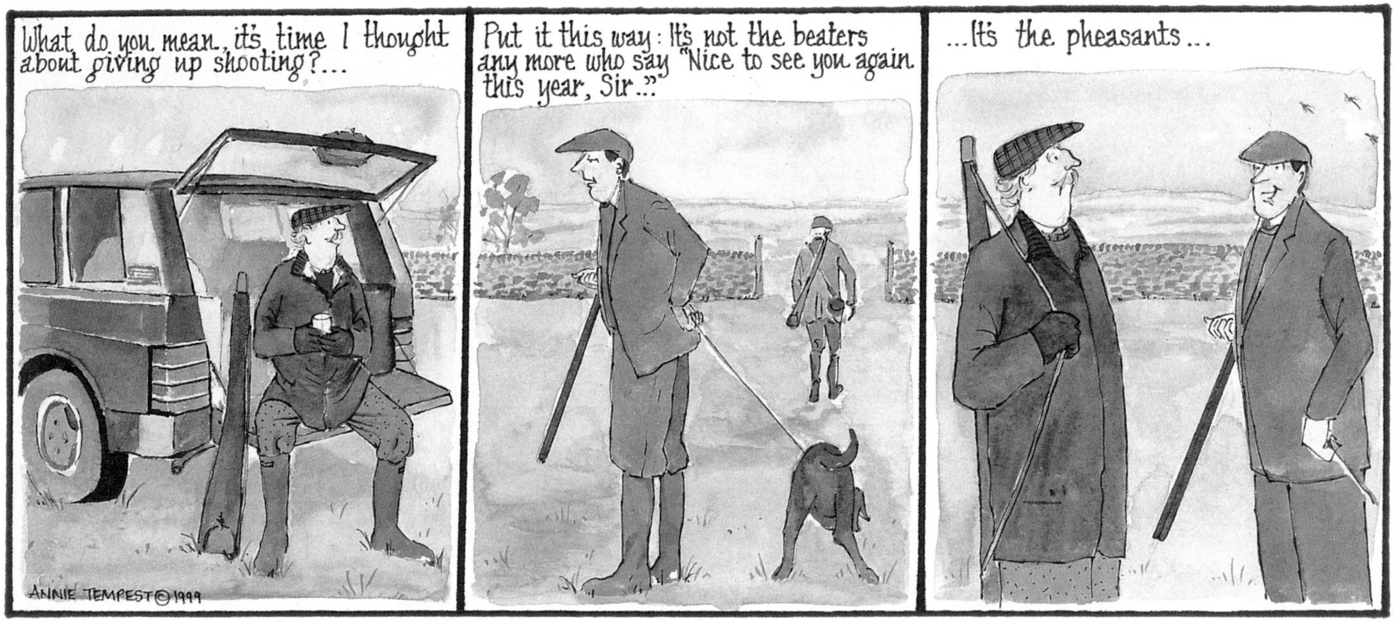
What do you mean, it's time I thought about giving up shooting?...
Put it this way: It's not the beaters any more who say "Nice to see you again this year, Sir..."
...It's the pheasants...
ANNIE TEMPEST © 1999

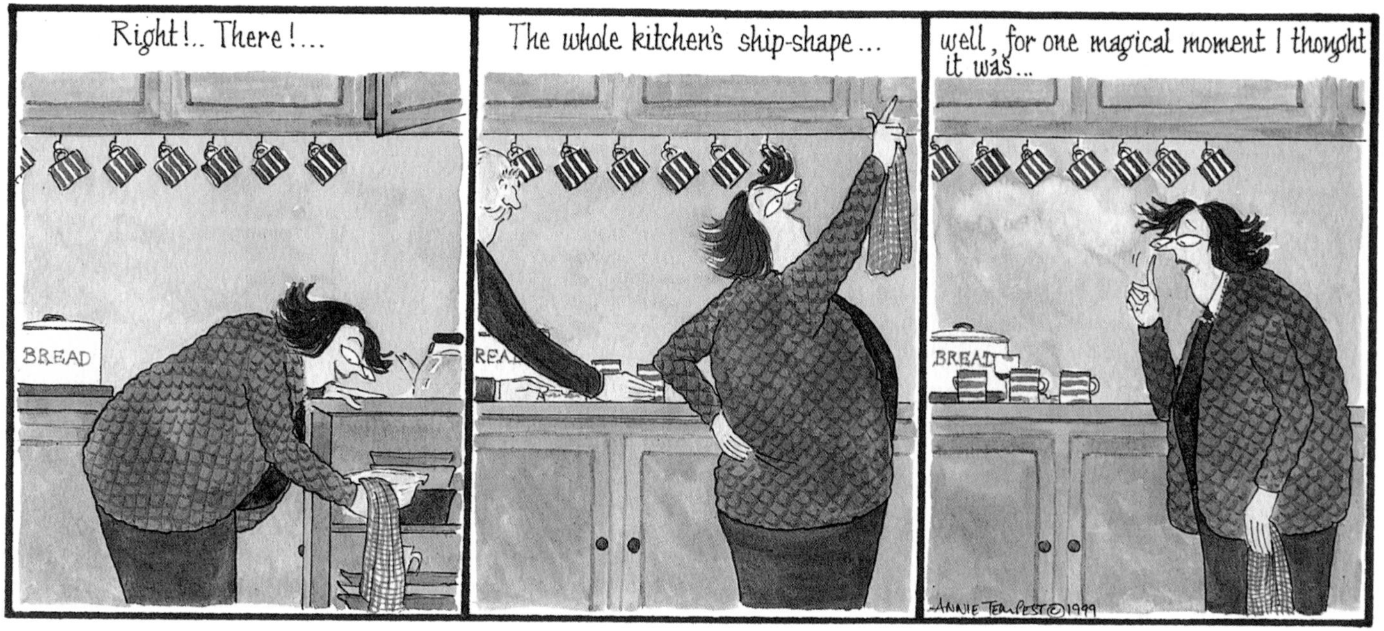
Right!.. There!...
The whole kitchen's ship-shape...
well, for one magical moment I thought it was...
BREAD
ANNIE TEMPEST © 1999

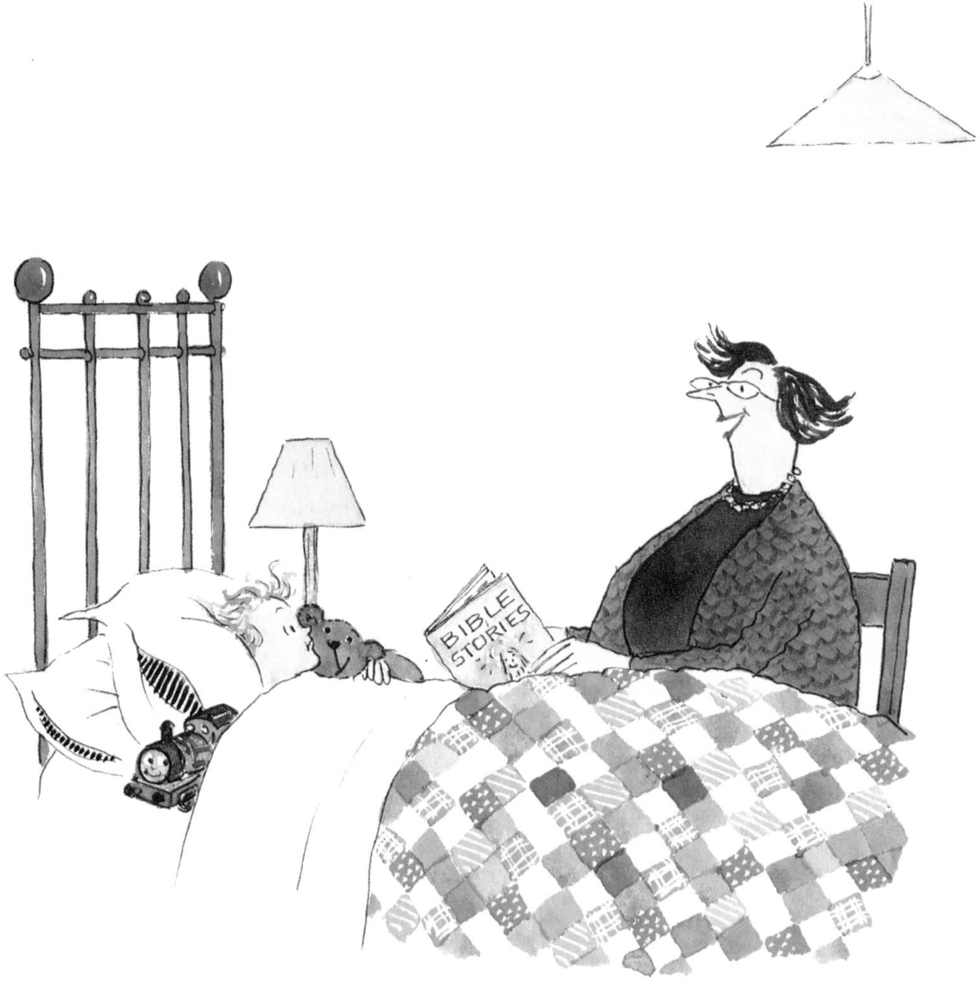
BIBLE STORIES

"I would imagine heaven's either in SW10 or SW3, wouldn't you?"

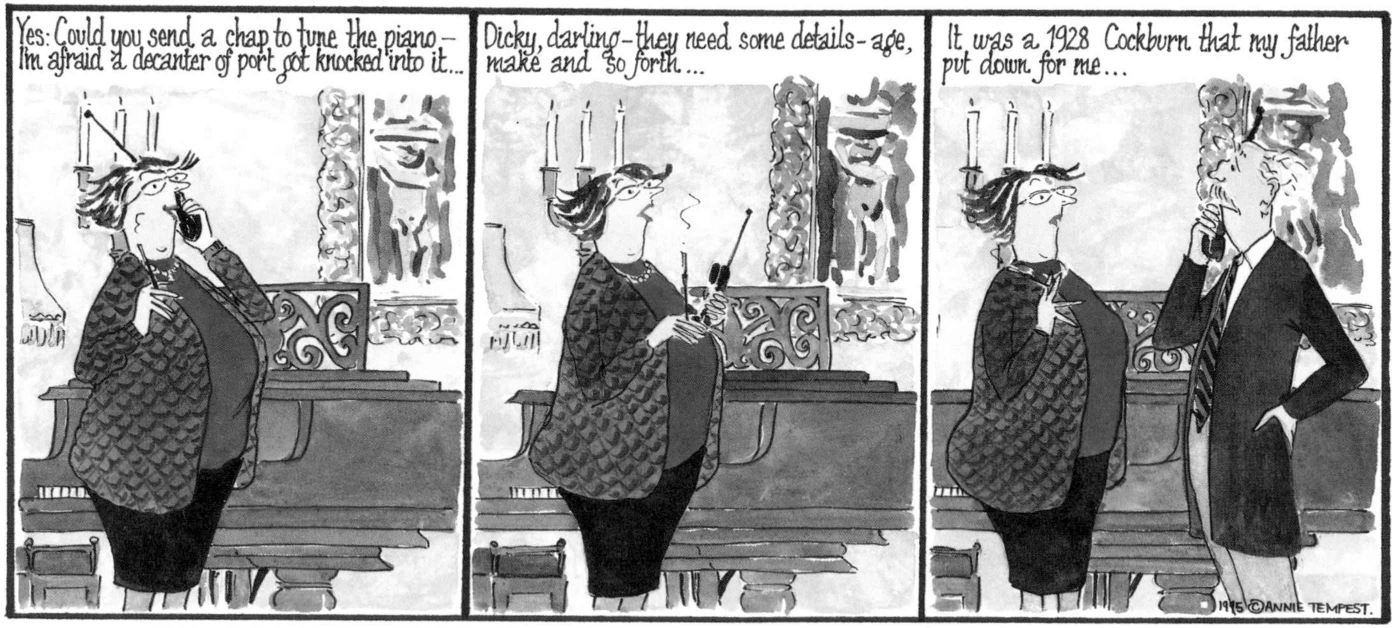
Yes: Could you send a chap to tune the piano - I'm afraid a decanter of port got knocked into it...
Dicky, darling - they need some details - age, make and so forth...
It was a 1928 Cockburn that my father put down for me...
1995 © ANNIE TEMPEST.

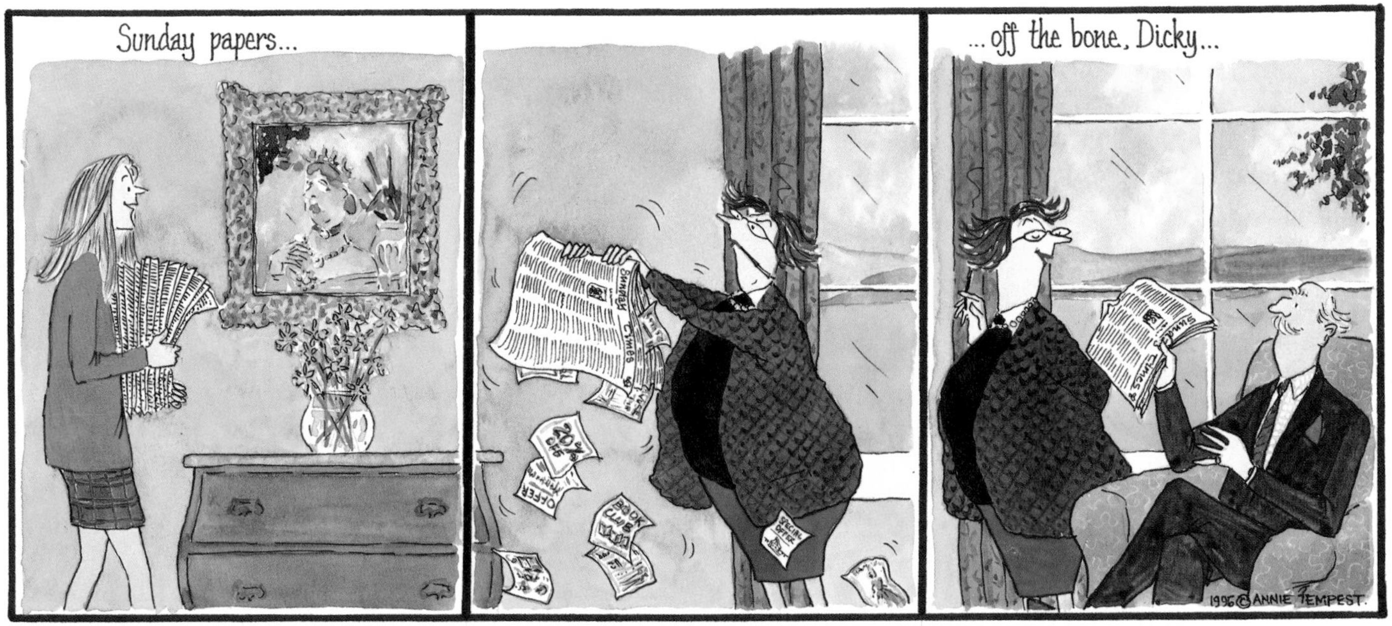
Sunday papers...
...off the bone, Dicky...
BOOK CLUB
SPECIAL OFFER
1996 © ANNIE TEMPEST.

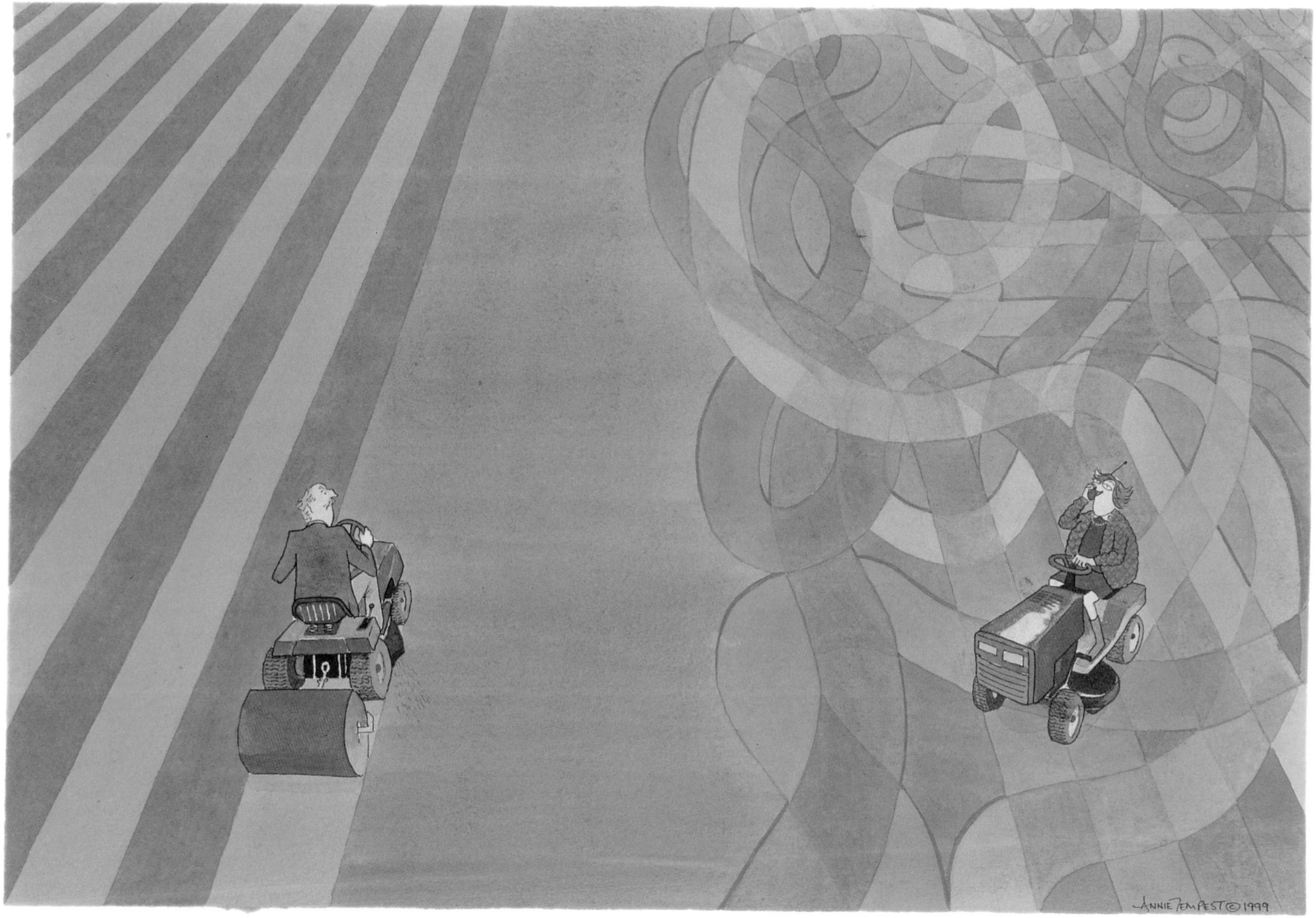
ANNIE TEMPEST © 1999

Mars and Venus mow the lawn . . .

Orion Books in association with The O'Shea Gallery announce
the future publication by Annie Tempest:

The Tottering-By-Gently Journal   *September 2002*

ANNIE TEMPEST

Tottering-By-Gently

Annie is one of Britain's best loved cartoonists. For her popular strip cartoon 'The Yuppies', which ran for seven years in the *Daily Mail*, she was recognized by her peers in the Cartoonists Club of Great Britain as 'Strip Cartoonist of the year'. In 1993 Annie embarked on her current internationally acclaimed cartoon strip, 'Tottering-By-Gently' for *Country Life*. In 1995 The O'Shea Gallery was appointed agent for Annie Tempest's originals and publisher of her books and prints. The Gallery promotes and exhibits Annie's work worldwide.

Tottering-By-Gently is a village in the fictional county of North Pimmshire, in which the big house, is inhabited by Lord and Lady Tottering, affectionately known as Daffy and Dicky. Through them and their extended family, Annie Tempest casts her gimlet eye over everything from inter-generational tensions and the differing perspectives of men and women, to field sports, diet, ageing, gardening, fashion, food, convention and much, much more. Her now large international following proves that she touches a note of universal truth in her beautifully executed and exquisitely detailed cartoons as she gently laughs with us at the stuff of life.

Annie tempest has had eight collections of her cartoons published and has worked for most of our national newspapers and life-style magazines over the last fifteen years. As Sir Roy Strong observed: "Annie Tempest has a great talent. She has the similar cult appeal of Osbert Lancaster and has created her characters from a certain set, but her observations are social as against political. They are gentler and beautifully observed. Annie Tempest is a bit of England – she articulates the things which set us apart and which form our identity".

Tottering-By-Gently

To receive information about Annie Tempest's original drawings, a catalogue of her signed numbered edition prints, up to date listings of *Tottering-By-Gently* publications, products and events, please contact:

Tottering-By-Gently, Twelve Acres, Valence, Nr. Westerham, Kent TN16 1QL
Tel: 01959 569301 Fax: 01959 569302
e.mail: osheagallery@paston.co.uk   website: http://www.tottering.com

All enquires relating to: *The Tottering-By-Gently Journal*
Please contact:

Orion Books, Orion House, 5 Upper Saint Martin's Lane, London WC2H 9EA
Tel: 020 7240 3444 Fax: 0207836 4266